Racing Pigeons

RACING PIGEONS

David Glover and
Marie Beaumont

The Crowood Press

First published in 1999 by
The Crowood Press Ltd
Ramsbury, Marlborough
Wiltshire SN8 2HR

www.crowood.com

This impression 2004

British Library Cataloguing in Publication Data
A catalogue record for this book is available from the British Library.

ISBN 1 86126 232 9

Illustrations by David Glover

Typeset by Phoenix Typesetting
Ilkley, West Yorkshire

Printed and bound in Great Britain by
CPI, Bath

CONTENTS

INTRODUCTION

There are many books and videos currently on the market covering the variety of methods that can lead to success in the sport of pigeon racing. What is, and has been, lacking for a long time is basic information and direction for those who are considering joining this sport, or for those existing fanciers who wish to increase their knowledge about any aspect of basic management. Many of today's pigeon fanciers have been raised in pigeon racing families and the management of a loft, breeding, racing and treatment of disease are second nature to them. Few stop to consider what needs to be passed on to the newcomer to the sport. On many occasions in our work with the pigeon racing magazine, *British Homing World*, we have been asked the same basic questions, and it is for this reason that we feel this book is necessary. Chapter by chapter we trace the origins of the modern racing pigeon, the development of the sport, the physiology of the pigeon, housing, breeding, feeding, various methods of racing and treatment of disease. We also hope to show the reader the tremendous pleasure and satisfaction to be gained from the ownership and racing of pigeons, either as an individual or as part of a family group.

We would like to record our thanks to Steve Spinks of Blackpool for his contribution to Chapter 9 on pigeon health.

David Glover and Marie Beaumont

1 A HISTORY OF THE SPORT

It is an indisputable fact that the modern day racing pigeon is a modified variant of the Rock dove, whose own origins stem from the dove so beloved by the ancients. One of the earliest records of the dove is to be found many thousands of years ago in the story of Noah and the flood. The folklore of all racial and religious groups includes the story of how a dove was released three times from the Ark, finally to return carrying a twig, signifying that the flood-water was receding. Records and carvings of doves have been found as early as 3000BC and, surprisingly, they bear a startling resemblance to the racing pigeons of today. That the homing instinct of the dove was strong is proven by an Egyptian bas-relief dated around 1350BC, which depicts a flock of doves being released from their cages to fly and then return. In fact, from the earliest times, there are many stories telling of the pigeon's homing instinct. The early Greek poets often alluded to ladies and gentlemen using doves to carry messages to and from their lovers, thus demonstrating the inter-relationship that existed between man and dove.

Over the ages different varieties of dove evolved, one of which was the Rock Dove. Slate-blue in colour, it does indeed bear a striking resemblance to the racing pigeon. It is believed that as various European and Asian civilizations declined or were destroyed by war, the domesticated doves were released from their cages to fend for themselves, finding shelter in hills or holes and crevices in rocks. Naturally, only the fittest survived to become known as Rock Doves. These were non-migratory birds and settled into a home for life, unless that home was endangered, whereupon a new home was sought and adopted. This versatile response to changing conditions accounts for its survival over other varieties which are now extinct. The Rock Dove was forced to range vast distances in search of food and water with the inevitable consequence that it would have to run the gamut of enemies – especially the falcon. Thus it had to develop speed, intelligence and endurance to avoid the enemy. It also had to develop its limited homing sense using sight and memory, the latter being especially important because it would not always be possible to arrive home, or leave, by the same route – a map of the surrounding countryside would have had to be built up in the brain. Hence the Rock Dove, ripe now for domestication.

The Birth of the Racing Pigeon

It is more than likely that the Far and Middle Eastern countries were the first to domesticate

An early Rock Dove.

An early fourteenth-century dovecote – the forerunner of a modern loft.

the Rock Dove, as ancient records depict the Japanese using pigeons as messengers to warn of earthquakes. The sending of first reports by pigeon, when the area was being devastated by earth tremors, would enable help to arrive as soon as possible. There are no records of the ancient Chinese using pigeons as messengers, although their upper classes certainly kept and bred them. Whistles of various pitches were attached to the pigeons, and, when they were in flight, the sound they made was tinkling and harmonious. On the other hand, whistles of discordant pitch were sometimes attached and the raucous noise was a deterrent to any unwelcome visitor, be it animal or human!

During an early Olympic Games in Greece, the use of the pigeon as a messenger of victories is well recorded. The first marathon runner was also a pigeon fancier and he took one of his hen birds which had young in the nest to the Games at Pisa in AD230. When the Greek scored his victory, he sent a message home via this hen bird, knowing that she would fly at the fastest possible speed to get home to her young. Thus, the villagers learned of the victory very quickly. The ancient Romans also had their messenger pigeons; while they were fighting and conquering the then known world, they used pigeons to report news of their victories to Rome.

By AD1100 and the time of the Persian Empire, the Sultan had pigeon lofts built in

Baghdad and other cities with the intention of providing a chain whereby news could be quickly transmitted from one end of the realm to the other.

The twelfth century was a time of exploration and travel, mainly by traders curious to see new lands, other customs and to gain a monopoly of trade with the East. The world was beginning to open up. Baghdad, being a great trading post on the East–West route, attracted a wide variety of nationalities, including many Western Europeans, such as Venetians, Belgians and Dutch. It was probably the Dutch sailors who, seeing the potential of the Persian homing pigeons, decided to take a few of these birds back with them. These were known as 'Baghdads' and it is assumed that the racing pigeons of the West are descendants of those Persian imports.

During the Middle Ages the Crusaders fought the Holy Wars, mainly in the Middle East, and this vast movement of warriors from the West to the East, crossing all the European lands, helped to spread the 'Baghdads' throughout Europe. Records show that the Crusaders used pigeons as messengers.

From then on, the pigeon became an increasingly familiar sight on the Western European landscape. Many pigeon lofts, or cotes, were built in England and France by rich landowners, usually sited near their castles or manor houses. At that time, pigeons were mainly used for food and they were housed firstly in cotes built of stone, soon to be replaced by the less expensive wood cotes. These were raised off the ground by pillars to protect the pigeons from damp and rodents and even had pan-tile roofs for air circulation. These early lofts were sheltered from the cold winds and invariably faced south.

In 1574, the Dutch were besieged at Leyden. Practically at the point of surrendering to the Spanish, the defenders made one last effort. They sent the swiftest pigeon they had with a message appealing for help. The bird got through in record time and help was speedily sent to save the Dutch. During the French–

Prussian war, pigeons also figured prominently as a means of communication, and were put to extensive use by the French during the siege of Paris. However, this did not prevent the Germans from winning the war as they used falcons and hawks to intercept these messengers.

By 1735 the English Carrier pigeon was well established, having evolved into a distinct breed that was very reliable over short distances but did not have a long range. It did, however, play a very small part in the development of the modern racing pigeon. The Eastern Carrier was also well established, spreading across Europe from east to west and, along with other varieties, was used by the Belgians to cultivate a pigeon with both homing ability and racing characteristics. During the early years of the nineteenth century, three distinct types of racing pigeons emerged in Belgium from three districts: (1) Antwerp; (2) Liège and Verviers; (3) Brussels.

In Antwerp the type which was eventually produced was a cross between the strains of Smerle, Cumulet and varieties of the English Carrier, called Horseman and Dragoon. The birds produced were, in essence, workers and could negotiate long distances successfully, being large, bold pigeons. At the same time, fanciers of the Liège and Verviers district produced their own type using the frilled Owl, Cumulet and Eastern Carrier, and the type of bird these produced were small, powerfully built pigeons.

Brussels, as the metropolis of the country, combined the two main types from the provinces and produced a pigeon which was broad and short. By this time the Belgians had almost universally adopted pigeon racing as a hobby, with the result that the three types listed were cross-bred, incorporating large pigeons with strong bones which were good at racing longer distances but had little speed, with smaller boned pigeons having endurance and speed.

As the sport of pigeon racing got underway in Belgium and competition increased, various fanciers with far-sighted vision and enthusiasm sought ways of improving and developing the speed of the racing pigeon by selective breeding. Monsieur Ulens was a pigeon breeder of the highest order, who for years conscientiously attempted various cross-breeding at his lofts in Antwerp. His patience and perseverance eventually paid off when he crossed the Persian Carrier, Cumulet and Smyter (about which, unfortunately, very little is known). Subsequently, these pigeons spread all over the country, establishing Monsieur Ulens as the founder of the modern racing pigeon.

The nineteenth century was a time of fluctuation and change for the world, due to the new era of steam and thus the advent of the railway. The arrival of this method of travel meant that people who had lived within a prescribed area now had the scope and means to broaden their horizons. Along with increased travel facilities came a widening of outlook and knowledge of the way other people in different countries lived and spent their leisure time. A reduction of working hours saw the increase of various sports, including pigeon racing, and in the quest for ever better pigeons, the 'new' racing fanciers of all countries turned their eyes towards Belgium and so this stock was exported throughout the world.

Early Antwerp pigeons.

The Rome Race

In the nineteenth century, the Belgians and other Europeans felt that a pigeon race of 750 to 850 miles was certainly not too far, and in 1856 a race from Rome was held by Belgian, French and German fanciers. This race was such a success that it was repeated in 1868, 1878 and 1887. The society 'Le St Esprit' of Liège organized the first race in 1856, a distance of 729 miles from Rome to Brussels. Liberation day was 22 July and 125 birds were given their freedom at 4am. After seven days the first pigeon arrived in Belgium and, in all, twelve birds were reported to have made it to their home lofts. Twelve years later, in 1868, the 'Le St Esprit' society organized another race from Rome, when 180 pigeons were again released on 22 July. The first bird arrived home at 1.55pm on 3 August; by 12 August all the birds had been reported as safely home. Ten years later, the third Rome race was organized, this time by the Sport Colombofile and the Federation of Brussels. On this occasion, no less than 1,101 fanciers were eager to try their chances. The pigeons were liberated at 5am on 23 July. Officially, the first bird home belonged to Monsieur Rey of Brussels, but a bird belonging to a German fancier who lived just outside the radius for competing had been

Dragoons, circa 1874.

reported home two days before the Rey pigeon. This unrecognized bird was the pigeon that a few years later was purchased by an English fancier named J. W. Logan, who was to become world-renowned amongst pigeon fanciers, and the bird became the famous 'Rome I'. Sixty pigeons eventually returned to their lofts from the race.

The races from Rome certainly fired the enthusiasm of the fanciers of that era, and in 1887 and 1888 two races were organized, the first by the 'Fanna' of Germany, which was a success for German fanciers, and the second by the editor of the French pigeon fanciers' magazine, *Le Revue Colombofile*. The imagination of every European fancier was stimulated and there was great excitement when the race was fixed for 30 June 1888. However, at the last minute the Italian government banned any racing from Rome. The French editor, never one to admit defeat, rescheduled the race to take place from a small town in Corsica, called Calvi. Monday 2 July saw 649 pigeons liberated in ideal racing conditons. Unfortunately, the weather in France deteriorated and worsened en route. Nearly everyone had given up hope of seeing a pigeon return, when on Tuesday at 3.16pm, the great Belgian fancier, Alexander Hansenne, gave out the news that one of his pigeons had arrived. Wednesday saw a second pigeon arrive for a Monsieur Loicq at 10.26am and another for Monsieur Ginkels at 11.52am. When the race closed, only sixty-nine pigeons had arrived.

During the nineteenth century there were many more long-distance races in Europe, and in Belgium in particular, because the interest was keen. The sport was developing and gathering momentum, with fanciers even keener to breed pigeons which would fly the extreme distances.

The Birth of the Sport in England

Before 1812, the sport of pigeon racing was non-existent in England. However, many commercial firms were already using the pigeon for communication, as these were the pre-telegraphic days when the pigeon was the only rapid conveyer of news in existence. Thus the English Carrier pigeon was born. On the whole, these pigeons only needed to cover a limited range of fifty miles, and so a big, heavy, muscular type of pigeon evolved, which only needed to rely on memory homing as it was used once or twice a week, regularly, throughout the year.

The commercial lofts were in use for several decades and the managers of these lofts selected and bred from the best of their Carriers. Some of the larger commercial firms, such as the Manchester cotton houses, had teams of pigeons flying directly from Manchester to London, instead of the relay teams that most businesses used. To achieve a team that would fly this greater distance, most of the big commercial enterprises imported stock from Belgium and the Netherlands, as these European pigeons were already flying greater distances than the English Carrier. Some London businesses even maintained teams for messenger work to and from the Continent. Naturally the managers of these lofts were very proud of their achievements and, as a result, rivalry sprang up, sometimes resulting in sporting challenges over far greater distances than the messenger service.

In 1819, thirty-six birds from Antwerp were liberated in London and twelve of these arrived at their home lofts the following day. Several years later, a group of merchants from Antwerp had a bet that their pigeons could fly from London to Antwerp in less than six hours. The bet was actually lost by fifteen minutes due to heavy rain, and only half the pigeons sent had arrived home by the fourth day.

On the Manchester to London flight many keen wagers were won and lost, and there was no keener adherent to pigeons than John Pilling of Rochdale in Lancashire, who ran a business called Pilling and Co. John was later to become one of the pioneers of long-distance racing in England.

The Blue Carrier, a product of experimental breeding in the late nineteenth century.

Eventually the telegraph arrived, and with it the inevitable decline of the commercial lofts. Many of the now redundant pigeons came into the possession of private individuals, but very few of these Carriers developed into successful racing pigeons as, although they had plenty of muscle, they did not have the stamina to fly for long hours. However, the Industrial Revolution had arrived and, of all the counties of England, none was more powerfully affected than Lancashire, the seat of the cotton trade and the principal source of national revenue. Plenty of work meant higher wages than the average for the rest of the country and pigeon racing was adopted with zeal and enthusiasm by the Lancastrians. In fact, Lancashire became the cradle of the sport in England.

Racing pigeons as a sport began with the establishment of small clubs to race 'sweeps', or short-distance races, usually taking place on Sunday mornings. These involved fanciers dashing through the streets after a pigeon had arrived home, carrying the pigeon by hand, or in a bag, to a designated place or club-house. The first fancier to arrive, with pigeon, was the winner. All great fun for the general public, who were highly amused to see these fanciers running to the club-house as, invariably, one or

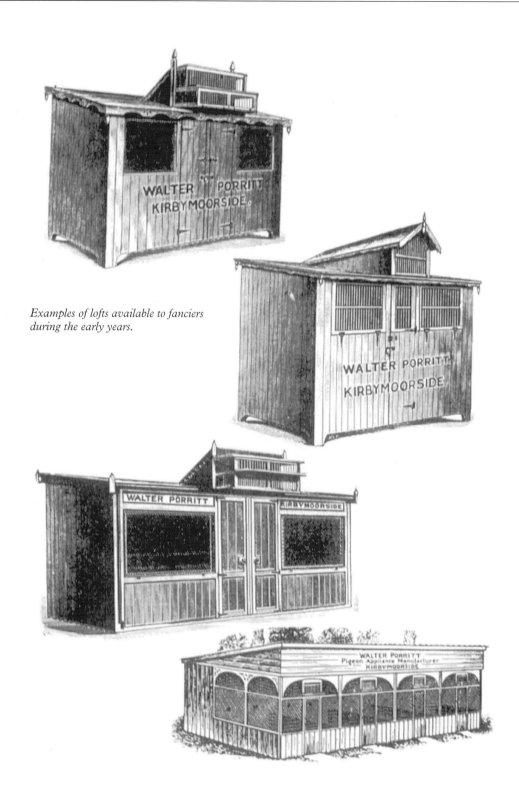

Examples of lofts available to fanciers during the early years.

two would collide in the club-house doorway and then the feathers would really fly!

Lofts were ramshackle affairs, with little provision for hygiene or ventilation and, in fact, the racing pigeons were usually housed in a box or crate, fixed to or against a back-yard wall. They were often kept in damp, overcrowded and draughty conditions, simply because fanciers of that time knew nothing better. They had absolutely no idea of the physiology of racing pigeons, nor even how to feed them properly. Even if those fanciers had known, the supply and variety of grain was limited. It is amazing that these early racing pigeons, fed on unsuitable grain and housed in such primitive conditions, were capable of achieving the performances they did.

More and more clubs were springing up and fanciers thought nothing of leaving home at 4am to walk two or three miles with a basket of pigeons, releasing them, walking back home for their arrival and then going to work at 6am. Scientists began to research the laws of heredity and men of wealth who were interested in the sport quickly realized that, for speed and stamina, the Belgian pigeons were far in advance of the English pigeons and so they began to import these Belgian birds into the country. In addition, with the advent of the railway in 1830, fanciers quickly realized the advantages of training pigeons using this method and this brought the idea of longer distance racing.

The sport was now beginning to take off nationally, and as fanciers became more aware of the beneficial effects of loft hygiene, the birds began to improve. Cleanliness was observed, a good system of ventilation was adopted and efforts were made to exclude damp and draughts from the lofts. Fanciers were even careful in their choice of site for the lofts as they tried to secure every advantage, realizing that a racing pigeon must be happy in its home if it was to show a keeness to return. A change also came about in the type of food and the system of feeding, as fanciers realized that their pigeons must be fed on grain, not only to derive energy but also to enable them to conserve that energy. Experiment and experience showed that the racing pigeon had needs which varied from season to season, therefore systematic feeding and a balanced diet became the order of the day.

The National Homing Union

As more and more people kept, bred and raced pigeons and clubs throughout the country continued to thrive, it became obvious that some sort of central body was necessary to nationalize the sport. In March 1896, a group of fanciers met in Leeds with the express purpose of forming a national body for the control of the sport, and this was to become a reality through the foresight and business acumen of a group of fanciers who had the interests of the sport at heart. Lancashire was represented at that meeting, and when, shortly afterwards, the Manchester Flying Club joined, the success of the fledgling institution was assured and the National Homing Union was formed.

Like most new organizations the Union made mistakes and it became apparent that a large body such as the council of the Homing Union, with limited time at its disposal, could not deal with the numerous problems that arose up and down the country. Tribunals were required to hear and sift the evidence of malpractice in the first instance, and it was decided that breaches of the rules should be dealt with by local centres before being taken, on appeal, to the national council for adjudication. Due to the sensible regulations laid down, such as checking malpractice, conditions of racing, suppression of shooting and trapping, and their general work in the best interests of the members, a rapid increase in membership was assured. The National Homing Union was instrumental in organizing rail transport to liberation sites for the affiliated clubs, and many hours were spent negotiating better travelling facilities for the racing pigeons. Identification of birds in those early days was a problem, as there was a percentage of members who would always be

'Mercury', awarded the Dickin Medal for carrying out a special task whilst serving with the Army Pigeon Service during World War II.

tempted to keep a good-looking stray should it land at their lofts, settle the pigeon to its new home and then race it. Therefore some means of identification became imperative. When the idea of identification rings was first proposed, along with the idea that the Union should issue them, it was combated by many fanciers who felt that a venture of this kind would result in the financial ruin of the Union; happily such gloomy forecasts proved untrue. A committee was formed to look into the desirability of timing devices to record the arrival of the bird at its home loft. The hard work, time and money spent, stimulated inventors to greater efforts, resulting in the production of the forerunners of the modern timing clock.

Members were exhorted to assist in building up strong union executives at the annual meetings, executives who possessed an understanding of the requirements of fanciers together with the ability and enthusiasm necessary for forcing ideas through the right channels to give a satisfactory outcome. It was generally felt that constructive criticism was essential for any undertaking to be successful, and this, coupled with the sinking of personal differences, would do much towards securing the unity of the general members.

Wartime Pigeons

The important role of pigeons during the two world wars is perhaps not generally known, but it is an undisputed fact that they saved thousands of lives during these two major conflicts. Their homing instinct plus ability, stamina and determination to arrive at the home loft was fully exploited by the military. During World War I it is estimated that the German troops commandeered over one million Belgian pigeons to be used for troop communication. Later, British, French, Italian and Belgian pigeons distinguished themselves by carrying messages under exceptionally difficult conditions which, when received, were of immense value to the war effort and, in many cases, led to the saving of lives.

Museums and archives in America, England and Germany contain numerous reports and citations to pigeons which displayed out-standing feats of gallantry during World War II. As in the previous war, this second global conflict saw the Germans once again commandeer pigeons for military use, not only from fanciers in Germany but also from the occupied countries, and it is estimated that the pigeons employed in Berlin alone, at the height of hostilities, were in the region of 60,000, with approximately 800 servicemen to manage them. The United States Army Pigeon Service employed around 54,000 pigeons managed by over 150 officers and approximately 3,000 other ranks.

The National Pigeon Service of Great Britain not only trained birds to be used on special missions and by the Resistance Movements of the Allies, but was also responsible for supplying young birds to the US Army Pigeon Service.

The war pigeons were trained to a high degree; some were even able to fly at night. They accompanied all branches of the military: field patrols, naval squadrons, including submarines, and air patrols. Parachutists also took them along for dropping out of bombers. This was accomplished by placing the pigeon in a paper bag with a hole in it, and the time needed for the pigeon to escape from the bag was sufficient to prevent it being killed by the suction of the aircraft. Some pigeons were equipped with cameras which took reconnaissance photographs of enemy targets and positions.

The Dickin Medal, established by Maria Dickin, founder of the People's Dispensary for

Men of the National Pigeon Service removing a message from a pigeon's leg during World War II.

Sick Animals, was popularly referred to as the 'animals VC'. This was awarded to any animal displaying conspicuous gallantry and devotion to duty associated with, or under the control of, any branch of the armed forces or Civil Defence units during World War II and its aftermath. The award was made only upon official recommendation and it is significant that of the fifty-three Dickin Medals awarded, eighteen were presented to dogs, three to horses, one to a cat and thirty-one to pigeons. The following three examples are representative of them all.

- 'White Vision' – Award, 2 December 1943: 'For delivering a message under exceptionally difficult conditions and so contributing to the rescue of an air crew while serving with the RAF in October 1943'. A flying-boat had to ditch in the Hebrides at 8.20 one morning; sea-rescue operations were hindered by very bad weather and an air search was impossible because of thick mist. At 5pm, White Vision arrived at her loft with a message giving the position of the ditched aircraft and, as a result, the search was resumed, the aircraft sighted and rescue of the crew effected. White Vision had flown sixty miles over heavy seas against a headwind of twenty-five miles an hour with visibility only a hundred yards at the place of release and three hundred yards at the home loft. A noble effort indeed!

- 'William of Orange' – Award, May 1945: 'For delivering a message from the Arnhem Airborne Operation in record time for any single pigeon, whilst serving with the APS in September 1944'. This pigeon was released at 4.30am with an important despatch and performed the unequalled feat of covering 260 miles – 135 of them over the sea – in four hours twenty-five minutes to his home loft. The flying speed was 1,740 yards per minute, nearly sixty miles an hour, showing great endurance and determination.

- 'Mercury' (ring no. NURP37CEN335) – Award, August 1946: 'For carrying out a special task involving a flight of 480 miles from northern Denmark whilst serving with the Special Section, Army Pigeon Service in July 1942'.

Decoding a message removed from a pigeon's leg during World War II.

English homing pigeons, circa 1878.

The years immediately following the Second World War were an exciting time for the sport, as scientific research gave the fanciers ever greater knowledge of the laws of heredity and genetics, enabling the experiments of these fanciers to move along more swiftly. As man in general is constantly seeking to improve, so the racing pigeon fraternity over the generations has gradually improved its stock. This improvement and development is still continuing today.

2 THE PIGEON

Unlike mammals, pigeons do not have external sex organs, and it is therefore very difficult to determine whether a young bird is a cock or a hen. The fancier has to rely on external characteristics and behaviour when the pigeon is a little older. However, there are some late maturing strains for which it may take a number of months before the sex can be confirmed.

The Cockbird

As the young cockbirds mature, it will be seen that they are usually of sturdy build, with broad, primary flight feathers (those at the extremity of the wing). They are aggressive, stronger and cheekier than the hen, enjoying indulgence in the courtship ritual and constantly trying to extend their territory. The eye ceres and beak wattles are usually more developed than the hen's, and, in the main, the head has a tendency to be dome-shaped.

The Henbird

The majority of hens are of a slimmer build than the cocks, with the primary flight feathers generally narrower. They are more considerate, especially when they have youngsters in the nest, and will defend their family devotedly. They enjoy the advances of the cocks and display this by dragging their tails and nodding their heads. They generally have less developed eye ceres and beak wattles but this is not always the case. The head is more rounded than that of a cockbird, often being slightly flat on top, but

again, as the racing pigeon becomes more refined, this characteristic is disappearing in some types.

The Skeleton

This is the framework of the body and protects the vital organs. The skull protects the brain and delicate organs, such as the hearing mechanism, whilst the ribs protect the heart, lungs, liver, stomach, kidneys and pancreas. However, strains vary in form and the skeleton is the basic cause for these differences, for example some breeds have shorter leg bones than others. Certain bones of the skeleton are solid, whilst others are hollow, or filled with marrow in which white blood cells are manufactured; some bones are like beads and others are long; some bones are connected by joints such as ball and socket joints (hip), hinge joints (knee), whilst others abut each other with a cushion between the bones, and there are even modifications of all three kinds of joint.

Each long bone comprises a shaft of brittle material with a covering of dense, hard bone, and around the whole is a skin-like substance called the periosteum which provides nourishment to the bone. If a bone terminates at a joint, the spongy end is a pad called the epiphyseal cartilage, which absorbs shocks. All through the bones there are small spaces which form tunnels to carry blood and nerves. The ribs, head bones and shoulder blades are flat and not as solid as they appear.

The most striking component of the pigeon's skeleton is the breastbone or sternum. This is

A pigeon skeleton.

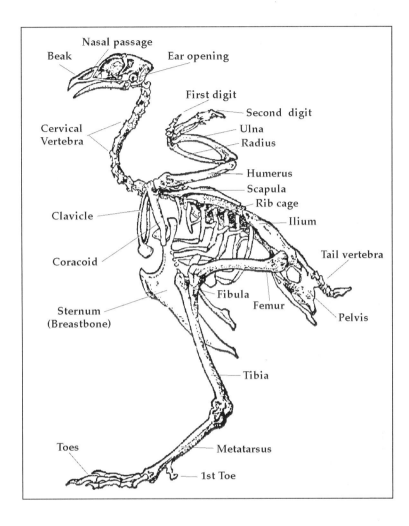

Nasal passage
Beak
Ear opening
First digit
Second digit
Cervical Vertebra
Ulna
Radius
Humerus
Scapula
Rib cage
Clavicle
Ilium
Coracoid
Tail vertebra
Fibula
Femur
Sternum (Breastbone)
Pelvis
Tibia
Toes
Metatarsus
1st Toe

not actually bone but a springy, tough cartilage which is flexible, as it needs to be, considering the strain it is put under. It is also deep, like a keel. At their lower extremities, the ribs join the sternum and where they meet enlargements are sometimes found which may remain throughout the pigeon's life, evidence that the bird was inadequately fed or was ailing for part of its growing period. The wings are similar to the arms of a human and they also have collar bones (clavicles).

Should a leg bone or wing fracture, it is in the interest of the fancier to understand the healing process, so that they can give the pigeon the required care. The bone ends have to be brought together and set, and these must knit. For several days the body will remove lime and other minerals from the bone ends, which then gradually soften. After this process the connecting fibres which are in the process of joining the bone ends together shrink, pulling the ends closer. This process takes about seven days and during this time it does not matter how straight the bone is kept as long as the ends are together. It is also possible to bend the bone at the break during this period; following this, the join is filled with calcium and phosphorus from the blood until it hardens. From this point on it is essential that the bone be kept straight by the use of some form of splint because, until the join is strong, the bone will not bend. Some broken bones set with what appears to be a bulge, but in time, as the junction shrinks, this largely disappears, leaving a stronger bone.

The skeleton is held together by the skeletal muscles, which co-operate with it in walking, flying, and so on. However, there are other muscles which are not seen outside the body and these are the smooth muscles. The skeletal muscles are striated (bands) under voluntary control, whilst the smooth muscles are not striated and assist in the functioning of the organs and digestive tract. Examples of smooth muscles are found in the gullet, intestines, bladder, blood vessels and sphincter, which are all involuntary muscles. Nourishment for the muscles is in the form of blood sugar, whilst the waste products are removed by the blood, leaving the body via the lungs and other excretory processes.

The Skin

Covering the whole framework of the skeleton is the skin, which itself consists of several layers, the two most important being the epidermis (outer layer) and the dermis (lower layer or true skin) which also consists of two layers. The skin constantly sheds and renews itself. Under the skin is subcutaneous connective tissue which is made up of elastic cells, through which run nerves, blood and lymph vessels. Fat is also often deposited here.

Feathers

Feathers grow out of the skin from follicles (sheaths) which contain small muscles that cause the bird's feathers to fluff out. There is great variation in plumage and colours among the different species of birds, but there are three basic types of colour. The first type is known as chemical-absorption colour, and such feathers are green, brown, red, orange or black in colour. These feathers absorb chemicals which, in some species, actually wash out when the bird takes a bath or has been out in rain. The second type is produced by the pigment in the ridges of the surface of the feathers and includes blue, green, yellow, or a combination of all three. The third type is the iridescent colouring seen on a pigeon's neck, which is metallic and produced by granules of pigment in the thin, transparent covering of the feathers.

Moulting of feathers is similar to the shedding of hair on mammals and this is discussed in detail on page 33.

The skin under the feathers produces oil and pigeons also have an oil gland at the base of the tail, the oil being spread to the feathers by the actions of the bird. When preening, the pigeon reaches round to the middle of its back, at the base of the tail, and then preens its feathers with its beak. It is believed that it pinches the gland to stimulate the release of the oil, which, when spread over the feathers, gives them a water-resistant coating and also helps to waterproof the skin. However, the skin is not resistant to all oils and some can soak through.

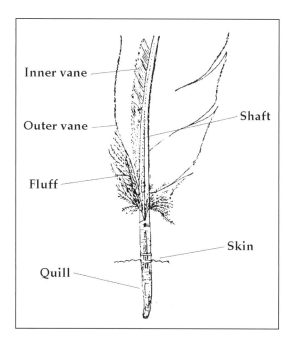

The structure of a feather.

As well as being a protective covering, the skin is sensitive to touch and pigeons respond through it to variations in temperature. If the skin is injured, it heals from the lower layers outwards, if not wholly destroyed. The sides of the injured area should be drawn together as closely as possible, because otherwise there will be a bare patch of skin which has neither glands nor feathers. As in humans, pigeons control their body temperature by sweating and there is a considerable loss of heat by water vapourization. So, a breeze which evaporates even a small amount of sweat produces a chilling effect. This goes on in the lungs of pigeons and helps to regulate the temperature as pigeons sweat internally, releasing water vapour into the lungs and air sacs. Two thirds of water loss occurs from the intestines and one third from the skin, lungs, air sacs, muscles and liver, but only the water loss from the skin and lungs reduces the body temperature. Therefore, when in flight, the pigeon uses a greater volume of water.

The Wings

Obviously, these are amongst the most important physical features of a racing pigeon, as they have to propel the pigeon over many miles and often through difficult conditions. The bones of the wing are hollow and filled with air, giving the pigeon buoyancy and an appreciable saving in weight. The wing is built up of feathers, arranged to produce an efficient mechanism for flight. Each individual wing feather is made up of keratin (a chemical which has a composition similar to the horns of cattle or hooves of horses) and consists of a stout, main shaft from which radiate smaller shafts (barbs) which, in turn, support fine structures (barbules). The whole is connected by a series of hooks and eyes which interlock the whole system and give the wing great flexibility.

The main wing feathers are known as flights, each wing carrying ten primary and ten secondary flights. The rest of the wing is made up of softer feathers called upper- and under-wing coverts. When it is spread open, the wing forms a rigid, light structure, rounded on top. To launch itself into flight, the pigeon uses the well-developed pectoral muscles which are attached to the edges of the breastbone (sternum) and to the wishbone (clavicle) and run to the top of the main wing bone (humerus). The lesser pectoral muscles move the wing upward and the great pectoral muscles bring the wing down – an activity which requires a great burst of energy. This muscle movement, combined with the speed at which the air passes over the upper- and the underside of the wing, creates an upward pressure and the pigeon is in flight. As it rises, depending on the airflow, the

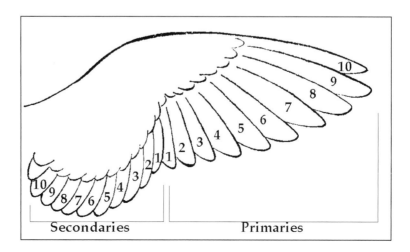

Primary and secondary feathers.

pigeon changes the angle of its wing to accommodate these air currents.

There is a wonderful arrangement in the wing which prevents stalling and this is the 'bastard' wing (alula) which consists of one main feather overlaid by one or two smaller ones to give it rigidity. The pigeon spreads this 'bastard' wing when in danger of stalling and the air flow above the wing is restored – a similar principle to that employed by the 'flaps' on an aeroplane wing.

The Nervous System

The brain is the centre from which nerves radiate and these can be likened to telegraph wires spreading throughout the body along several pathways, the principal part being the spinal cord. Most conscious body movements are regulated by the brain and spinal cord which are both well protected by the skull and the spine respectively. Nerves carry impulses to the brain from the most distant parts of the body. For example, feeling is a function of the nerves of the skin – sensitivity to temperature, wetness, dryness, sharpness, and so on. Suppose a pigeon touches a hot object. Its sense organs tell the brain – with the speed of light – and instantly the muscles receive an impulse which makes them contract and withdraw the body part from the hot object.

As well as the spinal cord pathway, other nerves leave the brain, running to organs and other parts of the body. The nerves in the spinal cord and the cranial nerves control the whole of the body; for every sensitive area in the pigeon there is a corresponding centre in the brain. As well as conscious responses to stimuli, there are also automatic responses. For instance, when a pigeon feels the urge to scratch a certain part of its body, the lifting of its leg to do this is automatic and is known as a reflex action. This is similar to a knee jerk in a human, which is also a pure reflex response.

The brain of a pigeon is smaller than our own, because the forepart (cerebrum) is smaller in the lower animals. This portion of the brain controls the willing, conscious actions, whilst the lower part (cerebellum) controls basic living functions. Pigeons can exist mechanically without the cerebrum but won't have the will to do anything – a vegetable-like existence. They will be able to breathe, eat if their heads are held over a food trough, sleep, wander aimlessly around and peck when hurt, but they will have no memory and be unable to learn or have the will to do anything. The cerebrum is the part of the brain which responds most to training. A pigeon cannot have its brain cluttered up by too much training; once it learns what is wanted from it and is properly rewarded, each new habit taught is easier to learn.

The Eye

Many fanciers adhere to the 'eye-sign' theory, believing that the eye holds the key to homing ability or some quality which enables one pigeon to surpass another in its capacity to reach home. There are those who breed their pigeons using 'eye-sign' as the basis. However, it will take quite some time before the new fancier can develop the ability to draw firm conclusions about health, intelligence and breeding ability from an inspection of the eye, and certainly this

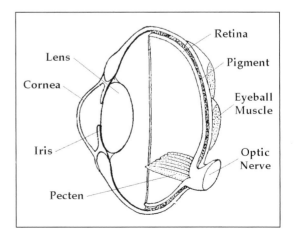

The eye.

cannot be gained from a superficial or hasty glance.

The eye is not as complicated and is much tougher than many people realize. It can be seen that the eye is a big, round transparent globe (cornea), and surrounding it is a ring of clear, white, glistening tissue (sclera). The tissue immediately surrounding the eye is the conjunctiva. Outside this, the lid is covered with cere, the amount of which varies according to breed and strains within breeds. In the middle of the eye is the pupil, which is an opening in the coloured circle of tissue known as the iris. The pupil becomes larger or smaller depending on the amount of light needed for vision, or on drug action or brain disease. A pigeon looking at a bright light has a very small pupil and, vice versa, when it becomes dark the pupil enlarges. The colour of the iris ranges from a pearl colour in some pigeons, yellow/greenish in others, blood colour in albinos, to dark brown or red/orange variations in others. The fluid in front of the iris and pupil (aqueous humour) is thin; the fluid behind (vitreous humour) is thicker.

Behind the pupil is the lens, which is tough and fibrous. As they pass through it, light rays are bent so that the image comes to rest on the sensitive area behind the lens (retina) which receives light impressions on the nerves embedded in it, which, in turn, transmit those impressions via the optic nerve to the brain.

The Ear

The ear begins with a hole in the head. By turning the head, sounds are captured which are then conducted inward through the external canal. The tube through which the sound passes terminates in a very delicate membrane – the eardrum. The rest of the ear is within the solid bone of the skull. Behind the drum is the columella, and a delicate mechanism communicates the vibrations or sounds registered by these bones to the nerves and thence to the brain.

The Nose

As far as is known, the pigeon's nose is one of its least developed sense organs. Besides breathing, little else is known of its use. As air is breathed in, it passes through the first part of a pair of cavities called the vestibule, then through a shelf-like arrangement of bones covered with tissue which can fill with blood. A mucous membrane covers this tissue. If the air breathed in is cold, the tissue fills with blood which helps to warm the air before it passes to the lungs. This tissue and arrangement of bones also filters the air breathed, removing dust and bacteria. Before pigeons can smell any odour (gas), these must be dissolved in the watery secretion which is present in the nose. Most animals, when they have the first stimulus of a new odour, begin to sniff, which, in turn, brings more of the odour into contact with the watery secretions in the nose, where it dissolves and the stimulation is increased. However, there is little evidence that pigeons use their noses in analyzing odours. Vision plays a far more important role in their lives.

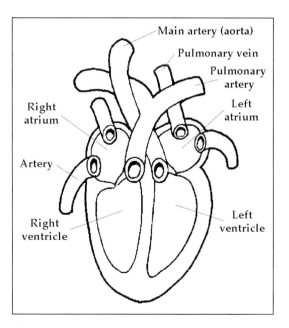

The circulatory system.

The Circulatory System

The body is nourished by the blood which delivers the nutrients needed to the cells. It also removes the toxins and waste products, delivering these to the excretory organs. The pump circulating the blood is the heart, which receives blood into two sides and then squeezes so that the blood is driven into two large tubes, one of which goes to the lungs, the other divides into smaller vessels carrying the blood all over the body.

In the lungs, the blood releases carbon dioxide to be exhaled, and then takes up oxygen which is transported back to the heart to be pumped round the body. Arteries carry the blood from the heart, starting in the main artery (aorta) and branching off into smaller and smaller arteries and then into the capillaries. From the capillaries, which exchange blood for waste, the veins pick up this waste and return it to the heart. The pigeon has a transverse vein in the neck connecting the two jugular veins. This is because the pigeon can turn its head almost 360 degrees, a twisting movement which can shut off the supply of blood through one jugular vein, necessitating a flow of blood from the constricted vein into the other. The pigeon's heart pumps about four ounces of blood per minute, so it has a much more rapid heartbeat than man. This is partly the reason why a pigeon has a much higher temperature than man (an average of 106°F compared with 98°F in man).

Blood comprises specialized cells in a specialized fluid known as plasma, that contains red cells for handling oxygen. When an artery is cut, the blood is seen to be bright red due to the oxygen, but when a vein is cut, because it is carrying less oxygen, the blood is seen to be darker. In experiments on poultry blood it was

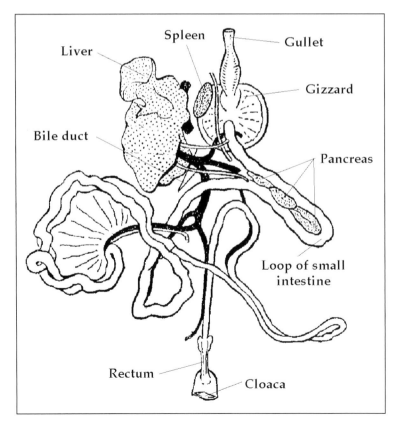

The digestive system.

found that the haemoglobin, which is rich in oxygen, increases when a hen is broody. If the same applies to pigeons, it would indicate why they race better when sitting, as the oxygen going to the tissues will be more abundant. Blood also contains white blood corpuscles which can engulf impurities and germs; platelets which help the blood to clot; and chemicals such as fibrin which, when a cut occurs, ferments with thrombin causing the fibrin to clot.

The main filter organ of the blood is the spleen, which is a long and narrow oval organ lying close to the stomach. Its prime purpose is purification of the blood, but it also manufactures both red and white cells.

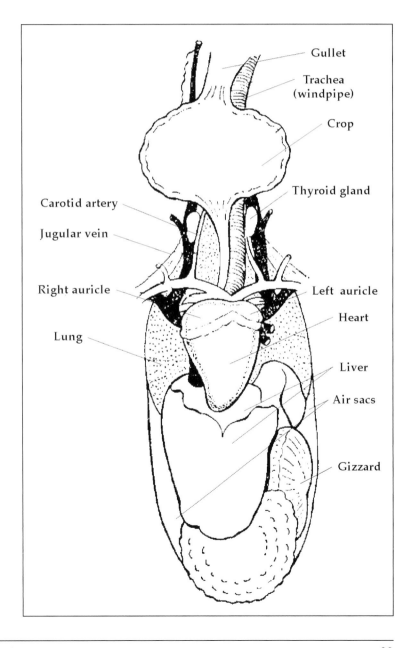

The respiratory system.

The Respiratory System

This is the means of supplying oxygen to the blood, removing waste and, to a degree, controlling body temperature. Air is taken from the nostrils to the throat, into the windpipe and finally into air sacs which force air into the lungs. There is a belief amongst pigeon fanciers that if a bird feels light in the hand, it is in good racing condition. True or not, it is a fact that pigeons, and indeed birds in general, have a large number of air sacs compared to other animals. It is the expansion and contraction of these air sacs that forces air into the lungs. When inflated during flight, the air sac reduces the density of the pigeon and helps it to remain airborne. The sacs also have a cooling function as heat is absorbed by the air sacs and expelled through the open beak through panting.

The Digestive System

The digestive system controls the nourishment that is transported by the blood around the body. Pigeons apparently have sensitive nerves in their beaks which enable them to distinguish between objects which look alike but are not, such as pebbles and grains. However, it is not known at this time how or why pigeons select certain grains and reject others; what part sight or taste plays has not been determined. To swallow, a pigeon stretches its neck and jerks its head, and by tongue pressure food goes down the gullet where it is mixed with saliva. It then enters the crop where it is softened but not digested.

Interestingly, both the cock and hen have the unique ability to produce 'milk' in the crop. The external layer of the crop lining becomes laden with fat and these cells are shed in the crop and turn to 'milk' – a protein and fat mix, which is then fed to the young. Below the crop is more gullet through which the food passes into the stomach to be coated with digestive juices. From there it travels into the gizzard, where it is ground. This is a wonderful organ in that it has walls so tough they don't wear out, even with grit and gravel rubbing the grain first into a powder after which it is soaked into a mush. As it moves into the intestines the food is further broken down into its component parts – carbohydrates, proteins, fats – so that they can pass through the intestinal walls into the lymph and blood.

The pancreas not only provides digestive juices, it also regulates the power of the body to handle sugar (glucose). In the pancreas are tiny islands which manufacture insulin, which in turn regulates blood sugar. If there is too much, it is stored in the liver; if too little, the pancreas recalls the sugar from the liver. During egg-laying, the number and size of the islands in the pancreas increases dramatically. If excess sugar has to be stored in the liver, it is first converted to glycogen (animal starch) and then, if needed, the liver releases the glucose from the conversion of the glycogen; thus the liver helps the pigeon in long-distance racing by releasing sugar to replace that which has been depleted. The liver also stores fat to be released when needed, in addition to the fat deposited in the tissues of the body.

The remnants of the food, after travelling through the intestines, are deposited through a valve into the cloaca and are then voided.

The Glandular System

By far the most important body regulator is the pituitary gland, located at the base of the brain. Its uses include:

- activating the mating instinct
- inciting broodiness
- helping sexual development
- affecting thought
- helping with the production of crop 'milk' in both male and female
- raising blood pressure.

If the gland is underactive it can cause fatness and stunt growth. One of the hormones in the pituitary gland is prolactin and this plays a big part in the production of crop 'milk'. It also increases the size and weight of the pancreas, liver and intestines so that digestive capacity and vitality are increased in the pigeon, which leads to a larger appetite so that the young are well fed. This explains why pigeons which are sitting race better.

The thyroid gland is found in the neck, on either side of the windpipe, the two parts not being connected as in many other species. The chemical, thyroxin, which contains about 60 per cent iodine, is secreted from it, therefore pigeons whose diets are deficient in iodine are more prone to sickness. The pigeon's metabolic rate has two peaks, one in the early morning and the other in the late afternoon. The metabolism of the pigeon also controls its temperature which is at its height when the metabolic rate is high. The temperature of a pigeon can vary from 105°F to 110°F. Pigeons have low heat production, can resist hunger and have a low calorie and food utilization, as the crop can store food for several hours. The pigeon can live for many days without sustenance.

The Reproductive System

The hen has only one ovary on the left-hand side, and from this an oviduct runs to the cloaca where the fertilized egg is passed. The fertilized

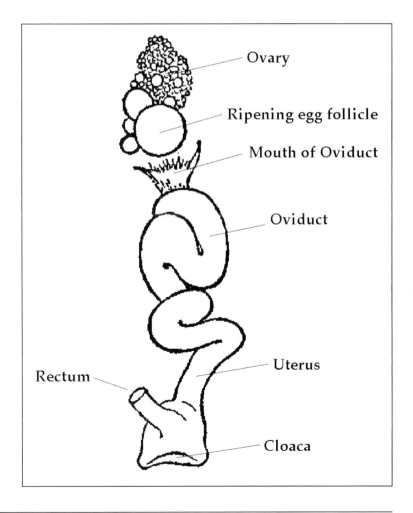

The reproductive system of a hen bird.

ovum and yolk leaves the ovary and begins its journey down the oviduct, accumulating egg white (albumen) which is secreted in the upper part of the oviduct. As it progresses down towards the cloaca, certain glands secrete a membranous coating on to the egg and this later forms the shell. Even before it is capable of reproducing, the ovary controls body development because, if it is removed, the hen tends to put on fat. The reproductive hormones can be activated by the presence of a mate, nestbowl or nestbox, and the sequence of driving, nest building, laying and sitting follows in due course. There is also an increase in the appetite of both mates.

The ovary is about the size and shape of a tic bean and contains the germ plasma of the pigeon – its genetic characteristics. Some of the cells grow slowly towards the surface, but when the birds are mated and driving to nest, the growth of the cells accelerates until they become follicles, which protrude out of the ovary until one bursts and the ovum is released. A second ovum leaves the ovary about two days later.

A change starts to take place in the bone marrow of the hen as calcium is removed and transported to the oviduct; after laying, calcium is removed from the food and transported back to the bones. This is why it is essential to give the pigeon extra calcium, either in the food or as grit, especially just before and during the breeding season.

The cockbird has two testicles located at the top of the abdomen, which enlarge during the breeding season, and copulation occurs when the cloaca of male and female are matched. Not only do the testicles produce sperm but they also secrete the male hormone, androgen, without which the cockbird, as a sire, would be ineffective as this produces the desire to mate.

The strong, domed head of a typical cock.

The Moult

The plumage of all birds, including pigeons, is in a constant state of renewal. This takes place gradually so that the pigeon can keep flying, but there is a certain time of the year when all the plumage is rapidly renewed. This is a very important part of the year as a good moult is the foundation for the following year's racing season. To see pigeons with large, bare patches on the head and neck can cause the new fancier anxiety and he or she may feel that the pigeons will never be fit to race again, but the moult is a perfectly natural part of the yearly cycle and should not give any cause for concern. Later, it will be found that the feathers have regrown and the pigeons will look much better with their new plumage.

The main moult (as opposed to the constant renewal of small body feathers) usually starts about the end of April and reaches its climax in September/October. It begins with the casting of the two first primary flights, one in each wing. The primary flights are the outside ten flights and the first of these, the innermost, is cast after the second round of eggs has been incubated for nine or ten days. However, if the birds are not mated until the end of March, the casting of these feathers will be delayed until May. As racing pigeons do not reach peak fitness until they have cast these first primaries, the new fancier is advised to pair his birds eight to nine weeks before racing begins. The two new flights usually take about four weeks to grow and, when they are nearly fully grown, the second pair of primaries are cast (those next to the innermost primaries). This usually occurs during the incubation of the third round of eggs, when the birds have again been sitting for nine or ten days. The casting of the next flight is

The rounded head of the hen bird, often slightly flattened on top.

sometimes delayed if a big youngster is being fed, but once the youngster is weaned, the parents will often cast two flights in each wing at the same time. In fact, old birds are usually racing when they are growing the first, second, third and even fourth primaries. The best wing condition for a pigeon which is racing is with the new primaries half grown, as the wing is then almost complete. If a flight is due to be cast, this can be a disadvantage to a racing bird as it has been likened to chewing with a loose tooth – uncomfortable and often painful.

Sometimes, a line will appear across the webbing of the growing primaries. This is known as a 'fret mark' and it is caused by the growing feathers being deprived of nourishment for a time, such as when a bird has a night away from the loft because it has not homed on race day. This can also occur when the bird has been in a hard race and has homed late on the day of release. If a pigeon misses a feed and all the energy has been concentrated on flying rather than on providing nourishment to the feather, this is sufficient to cause a fret mark. By observation of the primaries and any fret mark, depending on the position of the fret mark on

A bird in flight. Note that it is growing its last-but-one flight.

the flight, it is possible to determine which month of the racing season was hard for the bird. For example, a fret mark on the first primary indicates some hardship in May; on the second primary, June, and so on. When the fifth primary is cast, usually early August depending on when the birds were paired, the cover feathers, secondaries and tail feathers start to fall and the pigeon moults freely.

The secondaries are usually cast haphazardly, often two in each wing at the same time, with the pair nearest the body of the pigeon first, quickly followed, sometimes simultaneously, by the pair nearest the primaries, and the next pair follow suit until all are moulted. This applies to old birds, as young birds only moult two or three pairs of secondaries in each wing, leaving the rest unmoulted. Tail feathers are cast two at a time, but as this is very quick it is not unusual to see a pigeon with only six tail feathers. It is essential that pigeons have sufficient good food from August to December as this is the time when they are renewing the body feathering for the following year.

After the racing season closes most fanciers remove the hens from the cocks, keeping the hens in a separate compartment. By splitting the pairs it triggers the annual moult of the body feathers and the pigeons will go into a heavy moult during September/October. They should also have a regular bath in clean water and a little added salt is beneficial as this will clean any

breaks in the skin, whilst a pinch of copper sulphate dissolved in the water will prevent an outbreak of a condition known as feather rot. Exercise should not be forced at this time and the birds should be allowed to come and go as they please. Handling should be kept to an absolute minimum to avoid damaging growing feathers.

The end of November, early December should see the tenth (or end) primaries fully grown and this is when the moult is complete. Food quantity can be reduced as the birds will be spending most of their time roosting on their perches. During February, the old birds cast the small down feathers which give them heat during the winter, and these can be seen all over the loft; yearlings don't appear to cast these until later. Young birds cast their first primaries at around seven weeks old and continue moulting through the summer and into autumn – a period of about seven months. During their racing season (late July to middle of September) they are particularly bare of feathers round the neck and head and can have a gap in the tail, but this gap does not prevent them from flying.

The whole moulting period is a time in which a fancier needs to exercise common sense and not demand too much of birds which are growing so many feathers. If the bird is put under stress the feather quality will suffer and, as a consequence, the following season's racing results will be adversely affected.

3 BASIC MANAGEMENT

Acquiring Stock

In the process of building up a team of pigeons, the beginner is inclined to count on numbers. This is a big mistake as quality rather than quantity should be the aim; obtain quality and the numbers will take care of themselves. It follows that the new fancier should seek out a successful loft because it is there that a family of birds will have been established and proven itself over a number of years. An examination of the pedigrees of the stock pigeons will confirm that each generation has bred winners. It is also advisable to obtain birds from just one successful loft, as that fancier has obviously found a breeding pattern that produces winners. It would be foolish for the novice to obtain birds from here, there and everywhere and expect these, when mated, to produce winners. Never forget that winners paired to winners usually produce winners.

Many new fanciers think about purchasing young birds (March to May bred) but this can be a costly mistake as no successful fancier who is racing wants to part with his first- or second-round bred youngsters – he needs them himself. Likewise, no successful fancier wants to part with his best stock birds or racers, except for a very high price. Of course, there are quite a few commercial studs, which specialize in breeding good stock from sound, pedigree birds, and quite often youngsters can be purchased at a very reasonable cost. However, if purchasing from a racing loft, the logical answer is to acquire late-breds (July/August youngsters) which have been bred off pigeons which have won in the old bird season, thus keeping costs down and ensuring good foundation stock. Go to a local successful fancier, ask his advice and, if he is genuine, he will be only too willing to help and will usually pick youngsters that have the best chance of breeding winners. Listen to his ideas and management methods and don't hesitate to ask questions, however foolish they seem, as most old-hands like to see new fanciers in the making. It is more than likely that a beginner will not have handled many pigeons, so ask the successful fancier to show how it is done correctly.

Handling

Quite often, not enough attention is paid to the proper handling of pigeons. It is correct to assume that a pigeon is handled very much against its will, although some resent it less than others.

Obviously, when a pigeon is picked up, the main concern should be to convince the bird that the handler does not intend to harm it. Pass the bird slowly from one hand to the other with gentle stroking motions, rearranging any feathers that may have been disturbed by picking up the pigeon. When the beginner is more experienced they will be able to ascertain body formation, pectoral muscles, keel and vent by the sense of touch. Once the bird is settled in the hand, gently stretch out the wing – do not use force. First examine the upper surface of the wing which will show if there are any faults or blemishes in the small and large covering feathers. Then inspect the secondary flights, starting close to the body and working

A light-feed mixture of grains, high in carbohydrate.

outwards. Follow this by looking at the primaries, paying attention to the first three, as they can tell a story. The same can be said for the last three flights as they are often malformed in birds of doubtful health. After examining both wings, spread the tail feathers and check for defects. Finally, inspect the head and neck, looking for a clear, bright eye, spotless wattles, dry and clean beak and nostrils, feathers with long spindle ends and breathing that is steady and unhurried.

Handling may seem to be a difficult process but with practice it actually only takes a couple of minutes – watch an experienced fancier. Of course, there is a tremendous difference between handling a pigeon idly and handling it with all the senses alert. The beginner should learn to handle a pigeon in an alert manner right from the start, so that even when basketing for training, or race marking, these senses will come into play automatically and the owner will know immediately if something is not quite right physically.

Feeding

All living beings need adequate amounts of food containing a balanced measure of ingredients if they are to function successfully. Even though it is a proven fact that pigeons can digest animal protein, they are basically vegetarians, so by nature their staple diet is grain and some plant tissue. Successful feeding requires experience which is not possessed by the new pigeon fancier who does not know when the pigeon has had enough to eat.

In fact, many fanciers fail in their quest for success because they overfeed their birds and this is reflected in the bird's digestive organs. In the natural state, no bird finds itself consistently in an environment which has an abundance of food, but a pigeon fancier's birds have plenty of rich food for which they do not have to search or even wait. Overfeeding causes digestive disturbances by overloading and overworking the digestive organs, thereby reducing vitality and mental alertness. The temptation to throw down that extra handful of grain is great, but just a few grains extra can be too much and mean the difference between success and failure. There are, however, rough guides to follow, for example to stop feeding when the first bird stops eating and goes for a drink; or when it is noticed that the birds start to choose between one type of grain and another. Yet another guide is to feel the crops of the birds in the morning and, if these still contain food, they are getting too much to eat.

The art of feeding consists of giving the pigeons just sufficient food at one meal to last them until the next meal. This sounds simple but different fanciers have different methods of feeding their birds, usually developed by trial and error to suit each individual's requirements and management.

Hopper Feeding

Hopper feeding is when food is placed in a special trough (hopper) and is more or less kept in front of the birds all the time. The thinking behind this is that pigeons with food in front of them all the time do not eat as much as pigeons which are hand fed. Many successful fanciers hopper feed, especially prior to the longer races, but this often only works for certain pigeons – those which are naturally small eaters. If hopper fed using a mixture of grains a pigeon will, naturally, pick out the grains it likes best and scatter the others over the floor of the loft where they get fouled by excrement. On the whole, hopper-fed birds do not develop a healthy appetite and can become lazy, however many successful fanciers use the hopper method when they are only feeding one type of grain, for example beans, thus removing the bird's temptation to pick and choose its grains.

Hand Feeding

The other method of feeding is hand feeding, and the beginner must make up his mind as to

Maize, maples and white peas, plus dari and other small seeds, make up this standard high-protein mixture.

which method best suits his management. Basically, there is only half an ounce of food between a starvation diet and overfeeding, but to state that each pigeon needs a certain amount of food per day would be wrong, as pigeons are like any other animal: one day they may eat a lot and the next very little. Just like ourselves, if pigeons are active and interested in what they are doing they will have good appetites and look forward to their meals, and if they feel that they could have eaten just that little bit more, this will keep them active and interested and looking for the next meal.

The normal practice when feeding by hand is to feed twice a day, morning and evening, taking care to ensure that meals are at the same time each day. Hand feeding also gives the fancier the opportunity to observe his birds at close quarters, which will be helpful in the general loft management. At the first indication that they are going to be fed, every bird should be down on the floor or in that part of the loft where they

know they will be fed. If any bird does not show this keenness, there is something wrong with it, or with the fancier's feeding. Having said that, this is not an infallible rule, as when sitting, a keen hen or cock is reluctant to leave the nest, but in general, if a bird has always shown a healthy appetite and suddenly loses it, there is something wrong.

It is useful to put down 75 per cent of the feed to each compartment, or loft, leaving the birds to eat it up and then take a drink. Then feed the other 25 per cent very slowly, watching all the time how the birds eat. If they appear the least bit fussy, stop feeding at once. Whilst a pigeon may be looking for more immediately after being fed, an hour or two later the food will have swollen in the crop and it will be quite content. If in any doubt as to whether they are underfed it is a good idea to give them some beans. If they are genuinely hungry they will eat them immediately; if they toy with them, they have had enough. As a rough guide, an allowance of

A sample of French maize – the high carbohydrate content makes this a standard ingredient in many food mixtures.

between 1 and 1fioz (28 and 42g) per bird, per day is standard, depending on the weather. On some days they can do with less, on others a little more.

The little that pigeons can eat and survive on is truly amazing, but there is a difference between surviving and being fit and healthy to perform the tasks asked of them. Not only must the feed be controlled but the diet must be balanced. Correct feeding is necessary for:

- growth
- release of energy so that the body can function properly
- production of new and replacement of old tissue
- production of eggs and sperm.

These functions will be satisfactorily met by feeding a balanced diet which contains proteins, carbohydrates, fats, minerals, vitamins and water.

Food Content

Proteins

There are many kinds of proteins, but the vegetable proteins are those which closely relate to the pigeon's diet, and the richest sources are the legumes (beans, peas, tares and peanuts which have a very high percentage of protein) plus all vegetable matter. These proteins are composed of amino acids, of which there are over fifty different types, and therefore proteins can and do exist in many varieties; however no two proteins have the same composition. Even though there are over fifty different amino acids, only nine are known to be essential to pigeons, and when working out dietary values it is important to know the amino acids present as well as the protein analysis. For example, maize is high in a non-essential amino acid but low in tryptophane and lysine, both essential amino acids for growth, and therefore these can be added to a diet of maize to balance the diet. Pigeon feathers contain high levels of

A balanced mixture containing peas for protein, maize and smaller seed for carbohydrate – ideal for feeding youngsters.

cystine, so when the feathers are growing, cystine-rich food such as barley can be added to the diet.

A food containing 15 per cent protein is enough to rear youngsters but some successful fanciers believe that 20 per cent protein is necessary for more rapid growth. Maintenance food only needs 12 per cent protein to keep pigeons in excellent condition. Racers do not need high-protein foods before a race, but after a gruelling fly they do need high protein foods to build muscle. Crop 'milk' contains 58 per cent protein, so until the weaning stage, youngsters are already getting a high percentage to give them a good start in life. This also gives an indication of how much protein can be fed to the parents.

Carbohydrates

These come in the form of starch, and when eating seeds pigeons consume a high proportion of carbohydrates as starch is manufactured in the leaves of the plants which produced the seed. A plant leaf contains a substance called chlorophyll, much like haemoglobin which is contained in blood. This substance enables the leaf, using sunlight, to take oxygen from the air and combine it with water to make starch which is deposited in the plant tissues, including the seeds.

There are two types of carbohydrate – soluble and insoluble. The soluble carbohydrates are broken down into simple sugars and absorbed into the body to provide energy. If there is too much sugar present in the system, the excess is stored as fat. The insoluble carbohydrates are in the form of fibre, which is no use as a food. If too much fibre is present in the diet, it will affect the digestion of that diet. Grains rich in carbohydrates are: rice (unpolished) wheat, corn and maize, followed by barley and oats.

Fats

Fat is actually carbohydrate with most of the oxygen removed. Seeds contain much of the fat which a plant stores, and this gives sprouting seed its nourishment until it can manufacture its

A sample of barley – the main ingredient in many depurative mixes. Pigeons are reluctant to eat barley and will leave this grain in preference to others. If used in a mixture it is a good indicator that the birds have had sufficient to eat.

own substance from the air. Fat makes food rich and contains 2fi times the value that protein or carbohydrate can provide. When a pigeon consumes fat, say peanuts, it is stored in the body in its original form and, in time, the body converts it into pigeon fat. If, as is believed, a pigeon digests food as it flies, it would make sense to feed the pigeon a diet high in fat grains just prior to the race because they contain so much more energy than low-fat foods. Fats are also vehicles for vitamins A, D, E and K which are classed as fat-soluble vitamins.

Minerals

These are inorganic chemicals as opposed to the organic substances of proteins, carbohydrates and fat, and make up about 6 per cent of the pigeon's body; they are essential for its health. They are found in the following proportions: calcium (40 per cent), phosphorus (22 per cent), potassium (5 per cent), sulphur (4 per cent), chlorine (3 per cent), sodium (2 per cent) and magnesium (0.7 per cent). There are many other minerals which are needed in lesser amounts, such as iron, manganese, copper, iodine, zinc, cobalt, fluorine and boron.

Pigeons should have a supply of minerals available at all times. These are usually supplied to the birds in small unglazed gallipots which can be purchased from any pigeon store, whilst compound mixtures in the form of a fine powder containing all the essential minerals needed to develop a healthy pigeon can be obtained from a corn merchant. Minerals are hygroscopic and absorb moisture from the air and it is recommended that both minerals and grit are replaced on a daily basis. Provided they are clean and not contaminated, both grit and minerals can be taken into the house and left on a warm surface to dry out before reuse.

Calcium

Ninety per cent of body calcium is in the bones and 1 per cent in the circulation. It is needed for bone building; prevention of rickets; reproduction; muscle function; nerve function; and heart function. Sources include snail shells, oyster shells, alfalfa meal, milk and grains.

Tic beans – the standard content of high-protein mixes. They can be used exclusively and are useful if birds are to be hopper fed for a few days.

Despite the provision of nestboxes and bowls some hens will always nest on the floor using little or no nesting material.

Chlorine

Chlorine is found in combination with sodium and hydrogen. It is a component of gastric juice and urine, and helps to regulate the blood and body fluids. Source-food is ordinary salt.

Cobalt

A vitamin constituent concerned with growth and found in grains and greens grown in cobalt-rich soil.

Copper

Needed only in minute amounts. It forms haemoglobin with iron and is found in some grains and copper sulphate.

Iodine

Iodine is mainly found in the thyroid gland and is needed to help growth, regulate metabolism and prevent goitre. Source-foods include those grown in iodine-rich soil, shellfish, iodized salt and fish meal.

Iron

Iron is only needed in minute quantities for the red blood cells and transport of oxygen in blood. Source-grains include those from iron-rich soil.

Magnesium

Magnesium is only needed in minute amounts to help with muscle activity, bone-building, growth, nerve and blood function. It is found in foods grown in iodine-rich soil, iodized salt, shellfish and fish meal made from saltwater fish.

Phosphorus

Phosphorus is required for bone-building, carbohydrate and fat metabolism, to prevent rickets, as a component of blood and the liquid content of tissues. Sources include grains, oyster shells and ground bone but it is usually so abundant in the natural diet as to cause little concern.

Potassium

Potassium is found in blood and tissues. It helps to regulate body fluid, blood and muscular function, and is abundant in pigeon food.

Sodium

In combination with phosphorus, chlorine and sulphur in the body it helps to regulate body fluids and blood. It is a component of gastric juice and urine and is found in ordinary salt.

Sulphur

Only minute amounts are needed regularly. Sulphur regulates the body and combines with salts to form sulphates. It is found in any food containing protein.

Vitamins

A vitamin is one of a class of substances which exist in minute quantities in natural foods. They are necessary for normal nutrition and growth and their absence causes dietary disease. With a few exceptions all essential vitamins are present in a normal diet. It seems certain that pigeons can get all the vitamins they need from grains and sunshine, provided proper grains are fed and plenty of time is allowed for a pigeon to absorb the sunshine, especially during the winter months. The entire digestive tract produces vitamins in small quantities as a good

percentage of the digested mass in the lower bowel is bacteria which decomposes waste and synthesizes amino-acids and vitamins. In other words, bacteria produce vitamins. However, in disease conditions these bacteria cannot function as diarrhoea flushes them out, so in sickness it is essential that some vitamins are added to the diet.

Grit

Another essential requirement for the pigeon is grit, which is used to grind the food in the gizzard, and the new fancier will notice that pigeons, during the breeding cycle, eat copious amounts of grit. Again, there are many good commercial products available, some of which also combine black, powdered minerals. There are also mineral pick-stones available which can be left in the loft permanently.

The correct way to hold a pigeon.

Water

Water is absolutely essential to life, as everyone knows about the effects of dehydration. All experienced pigeon fanciers have seen the squeaker sitting about hunched up a few days after weaning, but after a good drink it quickly revives. Seventy per cent of a pigeon's body is water: blood transports all essential nutrients around the body to the cells and consists mainly of water, whilst water carries out all the waste products from the body and its evaporation from the skin controls temperature. Nearly all the water a pigeon drinks is absorbed and around 20 per cent is breathed out. In hot weather, as a pigeon pants and expels air very quickly, so it is expelling water, which has the effect of cooling the body. Nearly all the rest is passed in the urine.

The water content of food varies. Greens contain a lot of water, whilst certain grains contain very little. Water can transmit disease and that is why the water given to a pigeon should be clean and kept free from contamination by droppings. If there is no water supply, pigeons will leave their home environment in search of it and if a parent is deprived of water, regurgitation becomes difficult and growth in the youngsters is retarded. Pigeons prefer warm water to icy cold water, so in the winter, water-heating devices are useful.

Salt

Pigeons need salt and salt blocks can be supplied to them, or a little coarse salt left where the birds can reach it. They seem to know not to eat too much of this. Salt can also be put in the bath water and a pigeon will take a drink with no undue effects.

Feeding for Racing

When a pigeon is flying in a long-distance race, it is digesting food as it is flying – feel the crop of a bird just home from a 500-mile race. As every gram of fat turns into 2fi times as much energy as 1g of either protein or carbohydrate, high-fat foods should logically be given, but this is only for longer distance racing. The fat already stored in the liver and muscles is sufficient for a short race. For instance, in the athletic world a marathon runner consumes a high proportion of fat in the days leading up to a race, then large amounts of sugar for a quick energy boost in the final meal before the race. Foxhounds, who often run for very long hours at a stretch, and sled-dogs who do likewise, are also fed on a high-fat diet which keeps them going. As fat releases most energy per ounce, fanciers therefore choose high-fat foods for long-distance racing. For example, 1oz peanuts would supply nearly double the energy of 1oz maize because maize contains 8.9 per cent protein, 68.9 per cent carbohydrates and only 3.9 per cent fat, where-as peanuts contain 30.2 per cent protein, 11.6 per cent carbohydrate and 47.6 per cent fat.

For racing, fanciers need to find a way of feeding which will load the birds with stored nutrients, and the quickest way to fill the storage capacity of the liver and muscles is to feed enough protein (not more than 14 per cent) and see that the ration contains a high fat content with a reasonable amount of carbohydrates; some maize and a fairly large amount of oily seeds should be sufficient. There are many very good commercial mixtures on the market to cover all aspects of the pigeon year and, whilst these are slightly more costly than a home-made mix, they save time and provide all the nutrients needed at any particular time of the year.

Feeding for a Good Start in Life

Few fanciers realize the importance of proper feeding during the month before egg-laying. Every season, thousands of pigeon eggs fail to hatch and this is probably due to vitamin deficiency. Vitamins A and E are the most important, both being present in grain. Vitamin A is in the yellow pigment of maize and vitamin E is found in the germs of all grains. However, a lack of riboflavin is equally important and this is the first thing a fancier should think of if eggs fail to hatch. When the eggs move down the oviduct, they come to an area where riboflavin is added. If only grains are fed, there will be a deficiency of this nutrient and the eggs will not hatch. Green vegetable leaves are a rich source of vitamins as are newly sprouted grains. These should be added to the diet in the weeks before pairing and up to the time of egg-laying. It is essential that both grit and minerals are available to the birds at all times during this period.

Daily Management

The amount of time that the fancier spends with his birds each day depends on the time that he has available. Fanciers who have retired from work can spend many hours every day looking after their pigeons, whilst the working fancier's time is restricted by his working hours. Normally, the pigeons can be attended to every morning and evening. First thing in the morning the fancier will let the birds out for exercise whilst he cleans the loft and replenishes food and water. After exercise the birds will be called in for their food and then kept in the loft for the remainder of the day.

Some fanciers keep 'open hole' and allow their birds to leave and enter the loft at will, but this is only possible where there are no problems with cats or other predators and where the birds will not cause a problem for neighbours. Pigeons left sitting out on rooftops all day will never race successfully and will become a bad advertisement for the sport when they foul washing or rooftops. In general, the 'open hole' is only suitable in large or isolated gardens where birds will not cause friction.

Each evening the birds should be let out for

Examining the wing feathers.

exercise and again the fancier can attend to the daily tasks of cleaning the loft, replenishing water and topping up feeders whilst the birds enjoy their flight. Two exercise periods of one hour duration each day are sufficient to keep the birds in good condition, with additional exercise in the form of training tosses two or three times per week in the racing season.

Records

Several years ago, a very successful multi-millionaire businessman was asked to what he attributed his success. His reply was hard work, total dedication and, most importantly, attention to detail and not trusting to memory. These words are just as applicable to the pigeon

---

Pair No. .... Mated ....

Cock .... Ring No. ....

Strain ....

Hen .... Ring No. ....

Strain ....

First Egg	Hatched	Ring No.	Colour	Sex

Pair No. .... Mated ....

Cock .... Ring No. ....

Strain ....

Hen .... Ring No. ....

Strain ....

First Egg	Hatched	Ring No.	Colour	Sex

A page from a typical loft record book.

fancier. Pigeon racing is not a seasonal sport, to be enjoyed from March to September and then forgotten during the winter months. If anything, loft management has to be more absolute during the winter months, and what is accomplished during the dark days of winter has a great bearing on the success of the following season. This is the time when plans are laid for the following year, breeding pairs are sorted out, loft management overhauled, and candidates for the following year's races scrutinized.

However, all the good ideas in the world count for nothing if there are no facts from the previous season to back them up, and this is where loft records play such a big part. Any fancier can point out a winning pigeon to a visitor, but if pressed for details and there are no records, how can the fancier say for certain just how many prizes that pigeon has gained, how many training tosses it had, what the weather conditions were on race day, the condition of the bird, the wind direction, how the bird trapped? More importantly, loft records help a fancier to recognize a winning system and adhere to it. All the birds in the loft should be listed along with pedigrees and any winning performances so that future matings can be planned. When the matings are selected, a loft book, available from any supplier, should be used to record the details of parents and every youngster that is bred. It is also useful to have a wallchart pinned up in the loft with the details of pairings which can be transferred to the loft book as and when time allows. This also gives quick reference when considering candidates for the next race.

A race chart should also be filled in weekly for both old and young birds, so that information such as details of birds entered, race point, weather conditions, number of birds competing, nesting conditions, time of liberation, time of arrival, position taken and velocity can all be collated. This information will prove valuable not only for race candidates but for future matings. During the long winter nights a fancier can study his loft records which will not only provide him with valuable information but also, if racing was successful, activate some happy memories.

Wing Stamping

Under the rules of the Royal Pigeon Racing Association all pigeons entered in races have to carry a stamp on their wing with a contact address or telephone number should they become lost. A wing stamp can be purchased for a few pounds, however if the fancier does not possess a wing stamp the birds will be stamped by the club officials with the club stamp when the birds are marked for a race. Wing stamping of young birds is not painful but will obviously put them under some stress and therefore it is better to stamp them at home before going to the first race. Ideally, it is best to wing stamp them before their first flight, but this will be some weeks before their first race and the stamp will fade after several weekly baths. The best policy is to stamp them, or restamp them, several days before the first race.

Although lost birds can be traced through their ring number this has to be done through the Association's headquarters and it is much quicker if the finder can contact the owner of the bird directly via the telephone number on the wing stamp.

4 LOFT AND EQUIPMENT

Whatever the type of livestock, there is usually a specific name given to the accommodation provided for its well-being: chickens are kept in a chicken house or fowlpen; rabbits have a hutch; dogs have a kennel; and pigeons have their lofts. In certain areas of the country these lofts are known as dovecotes or kits. The term 'loft' probably reflects the fact that pigeons were originally kept in the attic or loft of a house and there are still many examples of attic pigeon lofts on the Continent. We do not know of any such examples in this country and doubt that planning authorities would allow such use in human dwellings.

There are many early dovecotes built in the grounds of great houses, and these were designed to allow the birds free flight from individual pigeonholes in the exterior of the building. The structures were usually brick, often circular, with a door and central area to allow the egg collector easy access to the nests. The birds kept in such cotes were of a different standard from the modern racing pigeon, meat and egg production being the main objective in their development.

Modern lofts come in any number of different styles and designs. Some are purpose-made designer lofts, whilst others are adaptations of buildings originally designed for other uses; some are massive structures costing thousands of pounds, whilst others are merely adapted garden sheds. One attraction of this sport is that, providing basic rules of ventilation and hygiene are employed, it matters little to the pigeon how much money the owner can afford to spend on the construction and design of the loft. In this sport members with limited income can compete on an equal footing with millionaires. Ever conscious of the need to promote pigeon racing to the fancier with a limited income we will endeavour to describe lofts and ancillary equipment that can be obtained for a few pounds alongside their more salubrious neighbours.

For the purpose of this book, we will only consider the ordinary back garden loft. The need for a loft that is in-keeping with the neighbourhood must be stressed. An unkempt shack

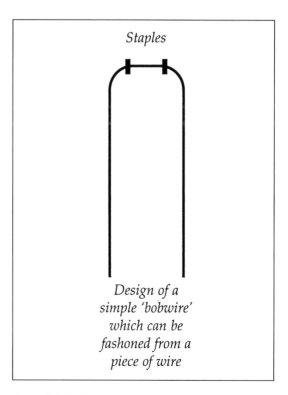

Staples

Design of a simple 'bobwire' which can be fashoned from a piece of wire

A simple bobwire.

made out of packing cases is an eyesore and will soon lead to friction. The two main factors that govern the size of the loft are the space available and the number of birds that it is intended to house. Err on the side of caution as, however good the intentions, it is very easy to end up with more pigeons than originally planned for. Uncrowded lofts with plenty of fresh air lead to healthy and contented birds.

Ventilation

Stale air incubates disease and to prevent this there should be a free flow of fresh air through the loft even when it is closed to the elements in the middle of winter. All lofts should be designed so that the internal air circulates, fresh air is introduced and stale air is expelled. There are several ways in which this can be achieved, and it is often a case of trial and error before the requirements of an individual loft are known. The underlying principles are that hot air rises and that the heat created by the pigeon's own body can be used to make the air circulate.

Two other factors must be considered when designing a loft. The structure must be designed so that the interior is dry at all times and the birds housed in a relatively draught-free environment. Using the rising air principle, there must be ventilation holes at the highest point to allow the rising, warm air to escape which will then cause fresh air to be sucked into the loft. If there are also ventilation holes at floor level, a steady flow of fresh air is achieved with stale air being forced out at the top and fresh air being introduced at the bottom.

From this it can be seen that the design of the roof is of great importance, and the more free air space over the area where the birds are housed the better. Traditional lofts had a sloping roof, but a more recent introduction has been the pan-tiled roof. Modern roof tiles allow plenty of gaps for stale air to escape whilst being completely watertight. In domestic housing the tiles are laid over a skin of roofing felt, but this should not be used for pigeon lofts. Such a skin would defeat the purpose of the tiles and prevent any movement of air between the gaps.

The prevention of severe draft is also of great

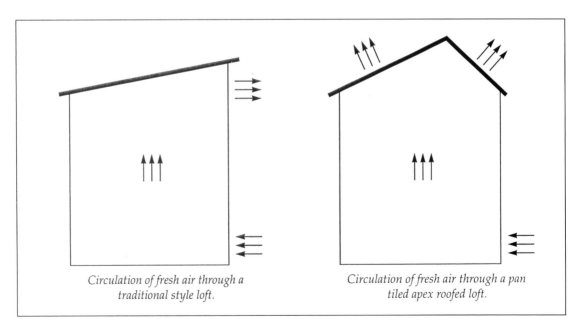

Circulation of fresh air through a traditional style loft.

Circulation of fresh air through a pan tiled apex roofed loft.

A plan of air circulation through the loft.

importance and the loft design should prevent the direct entry of cold air. The design of louvre windows is ideal for this and it is possible to buy purpose-made louvre panels that can be fitted to the outside of the loft to allow plenty of fresh air to enter without causing a draft. Ideally the loft should be designed so that the amount of ventilation can be varied at different times of the year and in different weather conditions. The test is, when the loft is closed up for the winter, ventilation should be maintained whilst preventing access for wind and rain.

There are many variations of loft design but all successful ones have good ventilation, a dry atmosphere and sufficient space for the number of birds housed. Purpose-built lofts can be purchased from a manufacturer and a number of these advertise regularly in pigeon magazines. They can be purchased complete with fittings and erected by the supplier. Additionally, ready-made second-hand lofts are often advertised, although the purchaser is usually required to remove and re-erect the loft themselves. All this is at a price and some will find it more rewarding to buy a basic structure and convert it to a loft. Rudimentary carpentry skills are the only requirement and the construction of a neat and tidy loft can, in itself, be as rewarding as racing the birds.

The newcomer to the sport will require what could be described as a 'starter' loft. He would usually be intending to keep about ten pairs of old birds and a loft in the region of 14ft x 6ft (430cm x 180cm) floor space would suffice. It would require a roof sloping from front to back and should be about 7ft (210cm) high at the front and 6ft (180cm) high at the back. The door is best placed at the side to allow plenty of space for trapping into two sections from the front. There are plenty of sectional wooden sheds of this size available from shed manufacturers.

The floor should be at least 8in (20cm) off the ground, with plenty of solid support underneath the cross timbers. Remember, it has to carry the fancier's weight and there should be no 'spring' in the floor when it is walked on. There should also be wire netting to prevent the birds from getting underneath the loft. Additionally, this

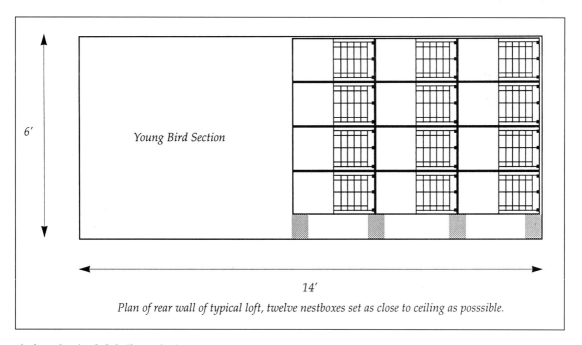

Plan of rear wall of typical loft, twelve nestboxes set as close to ceiling as posssible.

A plan of a simple loft (front view).

provides added security against cats, as underneath the loft is an ideal place for a cat to lie in wait for any unsuspecting bird that flies to the ground.

As a general rule there should be no ventilation holes in the back of the loft and, if possible, the loft should be positioned so that the back is facing north or east. This will keep out the bitterly cold north-east winds and allow the warm summer sun to filter into the loft via the traps at the front.

Creating a Pigeon Loft

Having purchased and erected the basic shed structure it must then be converted to a pigeon loft. For the following example, twelve nestboxes will be required, each measuring 30in x 15in x 15in (76cm x 38cm x 38cm) and these can either be purchased complete or constructed from fiin plywood. They are to be positioned on the back wall in four rows, three boxes to each row and they should be raised from the floor to be as near to the roof as possible, as pigeons always prefer to perch at a higher rather than a lower point. Although this example is only planning for ten pairs of birds it is always useful to have a spare couple of boxes where injured or sick pigeons can be locked away. The open space below the nestboxes is best boarded off to prevent the pigeons from going underneath where they are very difficult to catch. When making your own nestboxes it is better and probably cheaper to buy purpose-made fronts which contain the entry door and fittings that allow one side of the front to be folded back to split the box into two halves. The

A simple, basic loft converted from a garden shed.

use of this type of box eliminates the need for any other perches as the cocks will roost in the open side of the box whilst the hen is sitting on the nest. This also makes the cock more possessive of his own box and woe betide any other cock that dares to venture into his box. After all, it is his love for his nest and mate that motivates the pigeon to fly home in the fastest time possible.

Ventilation can be a simple row of 1in (2.5cm) diameter holes drilled into the side of the loft; one row at floor level and the other as close to the lip of the roof as possible. If such holes are used it is essential to cover the inside of them with small mesh to prevent the entry of vermin. A better method is to use moulded plastic louvre vents which can be purchased from any pigeon requisite supplier. These are usually about 22in x 12in (67cm x 30cm). A hole, slightly smaller than the size of the panel,

is cut from the wall of the loft and the louvre panels are simply screwed on to the outside of the loft to cover the hole.

Many fanciers believe that there cannot be too much fresh air entering the loft and their systems often consist of large panels of chicken wire let into the side or front. These are usually fanciers who are using the 'natural' system of racing, whereas the 'widowhood' flyers tend to have lofts in which the ventilation is restricted and more controllable (see Chapter 8). There are even lofts where the airflow can be adjusted by the use of sliding hardboard panels in the ceiling, controlled by levers at the front. The new fancier should remember that it is easier to start with a loft with restricted ventilation and then, by trial and error, alter the design to increase the airflow, than by doing the reverse and trying to restrict the airflow at a later date. The golden rule is that if there is a smell of

A small, purpose-made loft purchased from a specific loft manufacturer.

pigeons when entering the loft the ventilation is inadequate. The budding fancier would be well advised to visit as many lofts as possible to gain an idea of the amount of ventilation required before making any irreversible decisions.

Trapping Systems

It is not the time at which the bird appears in the sky that matters but the time at which the rubber is put into the clock, so it is essential to persuade the pigeon to enter the loft as quickly as possible for the fancier to remove the race rubber from its leg. It is only then that the race rubber can be 'clocked' and the time of arrival recorded. A bird arriving home from a race is in a state of nervous exhaustion and any unusual activity around the loft or change in the appearance of the loft or surroundings will make it even more nervous and less likely to enter and have the race rubber removed. The desire for

mate, food or water has to overcome its reluctance to be caught by the fancier.

Part of the loft must therefore be allocated for the entry of the birds and this also needs to be a one-way affair to prevent the bird from regaining its freedom once it has entered. A simple door will do and this is often the system employed by the 'widowhood' flyer. In the above example, the loft has a large, sliding front door which is kept wide open on race days. When the bird arrives he simply flies straight into the loft and into his nestbox. The fancier can follow the bird into the loft and close the door, preventing its escape. This sounds simple enough but problems can arise when a second bird arrives. After the initial arrival, the doors have to remain closed to keep the first bird in. Once it has eaten and taken a drink it will be looking to stretch its wings after the long flight, and when the door is opened to admit the

A typical Continental loft – the whole attic space of the house is used as a pigeon loft.

Plastic loft louvre screwed on to the outside of the loft.

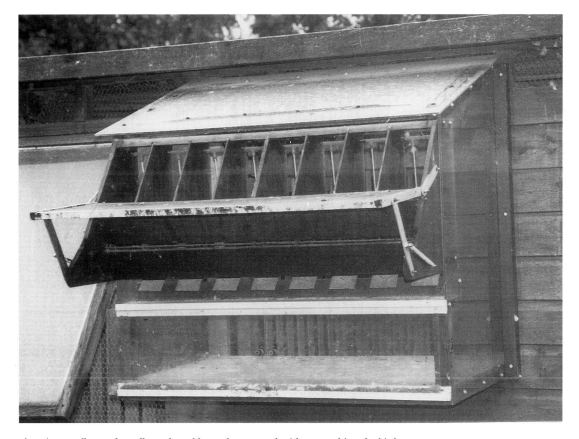

American stall trap that allows the rubber to be removed without catching the bird.

second arrival, the first one could take to the sky, startling the other bird into joining him. The second bird cannot win the race but there may still be prizes or pool money at stake, in which case the bird has to be caught, the rubber removed and then clocked.

A second problem with using open doors is how to allow entry for the late arrivals which come home after the fancier has left for the club. If doors are left open without the fancier present, it is an open invitation to cats which can quickly cause total devastation. If a cat gets into the loft it will not only kill, or maim, any bird that it can get hold of but it will also terrorize the rest of the birds. Pigeons frightened in this way will not race home, and it will be extremely difficult to get such birds into the loft after a cat attack. The same problem exists when birds are taken on training flights. Usually

this is done by the fancier himself and the bird's return journey is often faster than the car journey home. The birds arrive and go into the loft, eat any food that has been left for them and then fly about outside. This is training them to do the exact opposite of what is required in races, but there are few fanciers who can always be at home when birds arrive from training flights.

What is needed is a system whereby the birds can freely enter the loft but are restricted from re-emerging. Many fanciers use a dropboard, which is a level board fixed to the outside of the loft on which the birds are trained to land. Sometimes they will land on the roof of the loft but, after a little training, they will get into the habit of dropping directly on to the board. A hole is cut in the side of the loft at the level of this dropboard. The hole should be no more

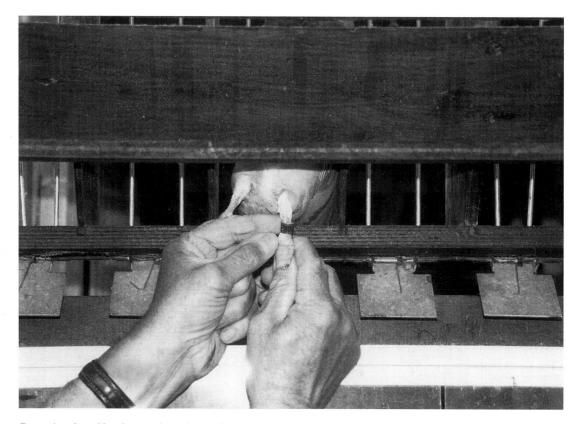

Removing the rubber from a pigeon in a stall trap.

than 9in (23cm) high and can be any width between 12in (30cm) and the full width of the dropboard. A small door is fitted on the inside of the loft, hinged at the top, to allow the hole to be covered from the elements when the trap is not in use. Also, on the internal wall and underneath the door are a set of 'bobwires' which allow birds to enter by pushing the wires open, and then drop back into place once the bird has flown on to the floor of the loft. As these wires are on the inside of the loft and slightly longer than the hole, they will only open inwards and, once they have dropped back into place, no bird can open them from the inside. The pigeons have to be trained to use these wires, but this is quite simple if it is done from their early days.

Young birds on the loft for the first time should be allowed to go in and out of the loft through the hole with the 'bobwires' fastened open. When they are confident and are going in and out through the hole, the wires should be dropped into place at a time when the birds are outside the loft and hungry. A few grains of corn scattered on to the loft floor quickly teaches them to push open the wires and fly into the loft.

There are many types of trapping devices, many developed and designed by individual fanciers to suit their own needs, but they must all allow for the bird that comes home when the fancier cannot be present. In recent years 'sputnik' traps have become popular and these are usually purchased directly from the manufacturer, either ready-made or in kit form. They are made of wood, plastic or aluminium and allow the birds to fly into the trap directly from inside the loft. This is particularly useful for young birds as yet unable to fly properly, which can be put into the trap and left in safety whilst

A standard sputnik trap.

they have a good look at the outside world and gain the bearings of their home loft location, an essential part of the education of a young bird.

On arrival from a race, the bird has to alight on to the loft roof or directly on to the 'sputnik'. It then enters the trap by dropping through the open bars and, if the fancier is quick enough, he can catch the bird whilst still in the trap, thereby saving valuable seconds. The disadvantage of the 'sputnik' is the same as with any other type of trap as the bird has to be trained to have confidence to enter. After experiencing what happens every week when it enters the trap, a nervous bird can become shy of trapping quickly and thus become a bad trapper. It is very important that the fancier does nothing to alarm the bird at the trapping stage as many birds become poor trappers due to the excited actions of the fancier rather than by the design of the trap.

Another recent development is the American stall trap. In many ways this is similar to a 'sputnik' in that the birds have to drop through an entry hole, the significant difference being that, with the stall trap, the bottom of the hole has a bobwire which, on race days, is locked shut. On normal training days this bobwire is left unlocked and the birds gain confidence by dropping into the hole and pushing the wire open to gain entry to the loft. When the wire is locked the bird drops into the hole and can go no further than the wire; neither can it go back and so it is trapped in that position until the fancier releases the bobwire. The bottom part of the slot is open and this allows the fancier to remove the race rubber without even catching the bird, saving time and unnecessary handling of the pigeon. These traps can be positioned at any height and they allow disabled fanciers, who are confined to wheelchairs, the joy of trapping and clocking their own pigeons. They are also

An example of a standard type of deep box perch with additional 'V' perches.

popular with fanciers who cannot always be at home on race days, as an inexperienced member of the family can easily clock the birds without the need to catch them.

Internal Design

The design of the interior of the loft can take all manner of shapes and sizes, usually dictated by the size and shape of the loft structure. Again, the following recommendations are the requirements of the simple 'starter' loft.

Sections

It is desirable that the old, mature birds are housed separately from the young birds, that is birds bred in the current year. In our typical loft it was decided that twelve nestboxes were required and, if placed in four rows of three boxes, they will occupy 7ft 6in (230cm) of the

length of the rear wall. The old bird compartment should therefore also be this width, as this will permit young birds a section which is 6ft 6in (200cm) wide in a 14ft (430cm) wide loft. The partition between the two compartments can be made from wooden battens with 2in (5cm) gaps between or can be a solid wall. A solid partition is preferable as, when battens are used, freshly weaned young birds will put their heads through the gaps and plead with their parents in the other section to feed them. Although it seems cruel at the time, the youngsters will progress more rapidly if left to fend for themselves and, once they have learned to feed and drink, they should have no further contact with their parents. A solid partition does not have to be substantial and can be made from battens and plywood, needing only sufficient strength to support a door.

A clay nestbowl.

Nestboxes

Pigeons will nest on any ledge or even on the floor, usually preferring a darkened corner where they can get away from the rest of the loft's inhabitants and claim a space of their own. If they are allowed to nest on the floor it is useful to provide some privacy for them. A piece of board leaning against the loft wall will suffice and the nesting pair will happily make the area under the arch their home. Although pigeons will nest virtually anywhere it is not always advisable to let them do as they please. Pigeons are generally intelligent birds but can be rather stupid when it comes to selecting a suitable nest site. On a smooth ledge, without a nestbowl, eggs will roll from the nest and break on the floor. When building a nest on the floor the birds will often select the most dangerous corner, such as behind a door which, when opened, could squash the bird and the eggs, or they may nest in an area where the fancier needs to walk, with the inherent danger of eggs being trampled on. Some pigeons will build large nest structures with straw or any other material that is available, whilst others are quite content to lay their eggs on two or three twigs, or pieces of straw, roughly placed together on the floor. Our experience is that it is better to maintain some discipline within the loft and not allow the pigeons to nest other than in the nestboxes provided, although there are several examples where champion pigeons have raced to a nest on the floor.

As with many items of equipment for pigeon racing, the nestbox can be cheap and simple or quite an elaborate affair. It needs to have

A disposable nestbowl made from pressed cardboard.

sufficient floorspace to allow room for a nest-bowl and two pigeons to stand in comfort. Headroom should be sufficient to allow the birds to stand without having to stoop, and also to copulate. During copulation the hen lowers her body to the floor to allow her mate to mount and this ritual is often carried out in the privacy of the nestbox. It is not that pigeons are shy about their mating, but if copulation takes place where other pigeons have access, some cocks may attempt to knock the cock from the hen, thus rendering the fertilization incomplete. The nestbox must have a door that can be fastened to lock the two birds inside the box. If widow-hood racing is being practised it is important that the box can be sectioned into two halves in order that the hen can be placed in the nestbowl with the cock locked in his own section in the box.

A typical nestbox would have a 30in x 20in (900 x 600cm) frontage with a depth of 16in (40cm). The sides would be solid with a grille on the front and a hinged door for entry. The box itself would be made of wood with the front made of either wood or plastic. The purpose-made plastic fronts are very useful and it is probably cheaper to buy these than make them.

Nestbowls

In their wild state, pigeons will scrape a small hollow on a rock ledge and construct their nest from a couple of twigs or feathers. In a domestic loft the birds will behave exactly the same and be quite content with a flat surface. This is not always the best practice for the fancier as, without a natural hollow in the floor, the eggs will often roll away and get broken. Rather than make hollows in the floor of the nestbox it is

A metal hopper feeder – this style allows the birds a good view of the grain and is very useful for feeding young birds after weaning.

more convenient to provide the birds with a bowl in which to build their nests. If straw is provided on the loft floor, some birds will build elaborate nests and seem to take delight in building a nest greater than their neighbours. Other pigeons appear lazy in this respect, being content with just a couple of feathers in the nest-bowl. The size of the structure does not appear to make any difference to the birds' racing or breeding abilities.

Clay nestbowls are the most popular with fanciers and can be purchased from pigeon equipment suppliers. They usually have at least one small hole in the bottom to allow for ventilation, and dust to fall out. Shallow, plastic nestbowls and throw-away fibre bowls are also available, the type used being the personal preference of the fancier. The birds will be just as happy to nest in a frame made from four pieces of wood, 10in x 2⁵⁄₈in x ⁵⁄₈in (25cm x 6cm x 1.25cm) and placed on the floor of the nest-box. A simple nestbowl can also be made by placing two housebricks at right angles to each other in the corner of the box.

Perches

Although it is sometimes necessary to provide perches in the old bird section of the loft, there is usually sufficient space available either in or on the nestboxes. This is the preferred arrangement as a cock will develop an affinity for his box if he roosts in it rather than on a separate perch. Normally, the hen will spend the night sitting eggs and, when she is not sitting, the cock will take her place.

In the young bird section it is necessary to

A wooden feeder – the roller on the top prevents the birds from standing on the feeder and fouling the grain.

supply plenty of perches and the number of these should always be greater than the number of young birds kept. A well-known phenomenon with young birds is the 'flyaway', when an entire team of birds take off from the loft with few of them ever being seen again. This is covered in greater depth in Chapter 7, but one of the possible causes of flyaways is overcrowding of young birds. The space available dictates the number of perches and the number of perches determines the number of birds that should be kept in that particular section. In our example, the young bird section should have at least thirty perches to enable a young bird team of twenty to twenty-five birds to be reared each season. The perches can be either the box type or saddle perch.

Box perches are the most popular as these allow the maximum number of perches in the limited space available. A box perch should be at least 10in x 10in x 8in (25cm x 25cm x 20cm). Sometimes they have a solid back or fit flush to the wall of the loft, whilst some fanciers prefer the perch to be set away from the wall on a batten, to allow a flow of air behind the perch. The gap between the wall and perch

A large water container. Note that it is sited on a heated stand that prevents the water from freezing in winter conditions.

should be no more than 1in (2.5cm) otherwise the droppings of the bird above will fall on to the bird below. Providing there is room for the bird to stand, the box perch can be as deep as the fancier wishes, and mature young birds bred early in the year will tend to mate and nest in deep box perches. This can be used as an incentive for the youngsters to race home, but some fanciers consider it strictly taboo to allow young birds to mate in their first year.

Saddle perches are usually made by joining two pieces of wood, 6in x 6in x 5in (15cm x 15cm x 13cm) at 45 degrees to each other. A problem with these perches is that they take up more space. Also, there is nothing to prevent the birds on the higher perches from soiling the feathers of the birds on the lower ones with their droppings. One advantage is that if these perches are used in a compartment for hens, it tends to stop the hens from mating together which can be a problem for the widowhood flyer where hens are kept separate from the cocks and have access to box perches or other possible sites for a nest.

Ancillary Equipment

With the loft constructed, fixtures and fittings complete, and the birds installed in their new home, further equipment is still needed before the birds can be successfully housed, trained

A standard five-pint water container.

and raced. They need basic food and water and this must be put before them in such a manner that it does not become soiled or contaminated. Some fanciers still throw the bird's food on to a clean floor, but even with the cleanest of floors there will be contamination of the food from the dust and diseases that are always present in the droppings. There are many feeding receptacles available that can be purchased at a reasonable price, but many fanciers prefer to construct their own from spare timber or utilize old household utensils.

Feeding Equipment

Feeders must be constructed to prevent, as far as possible, contamination from the birds' droppings. A simple feeder can be made from a trough, about 2ft (60cm) long with a lid to keep the contents clean. If the gap between the sides

of the trough and the lid is no more than 2fiin (6.5cm) wide the birds will not be able to get any part of their bodies, other than head and neck, into the feeder.

Water Drinkers

Again, these come in all sorts of shapes and sizes and household utensils can also be utilized to provide receptacles for clean water. Once again, they must be designed to prevent the birds from fouling the water and it is often cheaper and simpler to purchase a purpose-designed container for water. In the early days of the sport, a 2lb jam jar was the favourite water container and these cost nothing to obtain; two or three could be placed alongside the wall of the loft with a housebrick to support them. The brick will also provide a step for the birds to stand on when drinking. Drinkers are often sited on the

There are numerous types of small plastic water or food containers available at various prices.

loft floor but this allows dust and feathers to contaminate them. It is better to provide a ledge or shelf on which to stand the drinker to prevent this, but there must also be sufficient space on the shelf to allow the bird to stand whilst drinking.

Whatever type of drinkers are used it is essential that they are thoroughly cleaned every day and fresh, clean water provided. Once a week, each drinker should be washed and disinfected as contaminated water is a prime cause of disease. A simple but basic hygiene regime will prevent many problems.

Grit and Mineral Receptacles

As mentioned in Chapter 3, grit and minerals are essential requirements for healthy pigeons and these are usually provided in small gallipots. However, money can be saved by using small pots or jars from the kitchen. Metal containers should never be used for the storage of grit or minerals as there can be a chemical reaction with the metal and the contents would be contaminated. Glass or ceramic containers are ideal, but, especially when used for storing minerals, the contents can become damp due to water being carried from the drinker by the birds.

Cleaning Equipment

All animals and birds in captivity will defecate and it is necessary for the owner to take steps to remove the excrement. Many fanciers use some type of deep litter on the loft floor and this is only removed once or twice a year. The majority prefer to remove excrement on a regular basis, even cleaning the loft once or twice a day. This may appear to be a fairly arduous task, but if the

A standard training basket.

loft is cleaned on a regular basis it takes only a few minutes. If the excrement is allowed to accumulate it is obviously a much bigger job. Pigeons do not appear to have any preference as to the cleanliness of their surroundings and will be equally at home in a loft that is cleaned daily as in one that has deep litter which is only removed once a year. A clean loft is an object of pride for the owner and it is often this pride that provides the incentive to clean the loft rather than any great necessity for the welfare of the inhabitants.

Again, the basic tools can be purloined household items – a good yard brush and an implement for scraping the loft floor are basic. The scraper can be purchased from pigeon equipment suppliers, or a garden hoe or some similar tool could be used. It is also useful to have a small handbrush for brushing out the nestboxes and a small scraper for use on the perches and boxes. Other tools can be modified for particular jobs; a small paint scraper can be very useful for cleaning nestbowls and so on, whilst a dustpan and bucket are useful for the removal of waste.

There must also be some system for disposal of the excrement. If the fancier is a keen gardener this will not be a problem as pigeon droppings make excellent fertilizer. The gardener needs to be careful in this respect as fresh droppings are quite acidic and will burn tender crops if applied directly to the garden. However, if they are used on the compost heap they not only provide food for the garden but also help to rot down any other compost material. Garden compost produced this way should be left to stand for a year before it is used. It is better to have two compost heaps in use at

A standard 'V' perch.

the same time, one on which the fresh material is deposited and one from which the previous year's material is being used on the garden. In small gardens a compost heap is not always practical and there will be occasions when the amount of compost available exceeds the requirements of the garden. On allotments, other gardeners will no doubt be only too willing to receive an allocation of free compost material, but in the small back garden the disposal of droppings can be a problem. In many areas it can be disposed of with the household refuse or taken to a household waste collection point set up by the local council.

Baskets

Although pigeons usually travel by their own efforts, there are a number of occasions when they have to be transported by the fancier, for example when they are taken to the club

for race marking or transported to release points for training purposes. Obviously there is a need for some form of receptacle in which to carry the birds, the wicker training basket being the most popular. In the days when the railways were used for training and racing it was essential to use containers that were as lightweight as possible as the carriage charge was determined by weight. Wicker baskets are available in many shapes and sizes and are a sound investment for many years. They are hand-made and sold by specialist basket makers. They are quite expensive, however, if they are well treated with varnish and maintained in good condition they will survive many years of continuous use. One of the prime drawbacks of the wicker basket is that, due to the weave of the material, dust and debris can escape which can be a problem in the boot of the car. For this reason, many fanciers now

Ventilation bricks built in at floor level of the loft.

Grit can be supplied in a gallipot or merely placed on the wooden runners at the side of the loft. Here a small piece of wood has been nailed to the side runner to hold the grit.

A gallipot used to contain a supply of minerals which should be in front of the birds at all times.

prefer wooden crates which have solid bottoms and sides which help to reduce this problem. Most are home-made and can be designed to fit the boot of the fancier's own car.

Both of the aforementioned containers are designed to allow free movement of the pigeon, but there are occasions when this is not desirable. When pigeons are transported to shows it is helpful if the birds can be kept in their own compartments to avoid contact with other birds which may soil their feathers or even fight. Fighting is also a problem for the fancier taking a team of widowhood cocks to race marking, and many prefer a type of box which contains separate compartments. These can be made from the traditional wicker, whilst more modern ones are available constructed from pressed aluminium.

Electricity

Pigeons, being domesticated to this country, do not require any heat within the loft, even in the coldest of winters. However, there are many gadgets now available, all designed to make life easier for the fancier and enhance the welfare of the birds. Internal loft lighting is not essential but is very useful, especially for fanciers who work during the daytime and, during the shortened hours of winter daylight, can only tend to the birds in the darkness of the morning or night. To be able to switch on the electric light of the loft during the winter nights is a great asset and allows the birds to feed when the natural light is insufficient.

If electricity is available in the loft it can be put to many uses: loft vacuum cleaners, fresh air ionizers, cat deterrents and water heaters are all available on the commercial market and help to make life a little easier for the busy fancier.

A tidy pigeon loft can be an asset to the garden environment. If the loft is well maintained and freshly painted there will be no cause for complaint from family or neighbours and its appearance can be enhanced by climbing plants, flower borders and even hanging baskets. There is no more rewarding sight than a well-kept garden and loft with pigeons pecking about on a well-manicured lawn.

5 BREEDING

Selecting Pairs

If the novice has obtained stock from one fancier, in the first breeding season there should be no need to ponder the question: 'Which birds should I pair together?' The stock obtained will be from one family because a good fancier will have integrated stock so that they form his very own family. Therefore, although these youngsters are as yet unproven for the novice, selection will be easy when remembering the basic rule of breeding: 'pair like to like'. If there are any further doubts, the novice can approach the seller who will usually be only too willing to make suggested pairings.

Of course, successive seasons will present more of a challenge and need greater thought, but if the fancier keenly observes his birds during the racing season and keeps adequate records, never relying solely on memory, and remembers that 'pairing winners to winners produces winners', he won't go far wrong.

The offspring of every pairing is a combination of only part of each parent, so mating is something of a lottery. Many good racers, in combination with another, are incapable of passing on their qualities to the offspring, whilst sometimes a mediocre racing pigeon can breed good racing pigeons. These breeders are invaluable and it is vitally important to recognize them at an early stage. When selecting birds to breed from, fanciers should always look for birds which complement each other in every way. The mating of a long-distance winner with a shorter-distance performer will not improve either and should be avoided. A number of long-distance winners do pick up prizes at shorter distances, but usually the shorter-distance winner does not have the staying power to compete in the longer events. If pigeons are paired which are alike in every respect then it can be expected that the progeny will also be like the parents.

There are three distinct types of pairings: inbreeding, line-breeding and out-crossing.

Inbreeding
This is the closest relationship of all, for example brother to sister or father to daughter, and it has the effect of producing both the good and bad qualities of the ancestors, so the offspring will either be a superb specimen with few bad faults, or a faulty specimen with few good qualities which will invariably be lost in a race. It is good to inbreed occasionally to bring the bloodline back to purity, but several generations should elapse before repeating this procedure or a loss of stamina will be the result.

Line-Breeding
Line-breeding also involves family pairings, but not as closely as inbreeding. For example, grandsire to granddaughter, uncle to niece, half brother to half sister. These pairings can be carried on for generations, as the genes of a winning ancestor are then transmitted to both sides of the pedigree so there is, obviously, more chance of breeding a winner.

Out-Crossing
Many winners can be produced by this method – pairing two unrelated birds together – however if the offspring is paired to the offspring of another pair of unrelated pigeons, they very

rarely produce winners as the qualities of the original pigeons are diluted and lost. To correct this, the following generation should come from an inbred pairing to retain the qualities.

All fanciers should constantly be on the look-out for a breeder of winners and, if found, that pigeon should be kept for stock. Do not be tempted to race it, whether it be a cock or a hen, or whether it be a multiple prizewinner at national level or club level, as that pigeon is a goldmine and even the very best can be lost from a race; put it straight to stock! Good stock pigeons can produce winners for many years and bring the fancier continuous success.

Pairing Up

The traditional date for pairing up is 14 February (St Valentine's Day) and by the beginning of March most fanciers have their pigeons mated. Of course, experienced fanciers who race on different systems pair up much earlier, but for the novice the best time for pairing their pigeons is when sunny days begin to appear and Spring is on the way.

The first step is to get the nestboxes into position and the floors of the boxes covered with sand or similar material, to facilitate easy cleaning. Plenty of time must be allowed for the actual pairing up process and sometimes a great deal of patience is needed. Put each cock into a box and shut them in. Allow a few minutes for them to get used to the box and then put each hen into the box, one at a time. It is wise, at this time, to spend a few minutes watching each pair to make sure they take to each other. Sometimes a young hen can be unwilling to pair because she is not used to the confinement of the nestbox, and the cock may become vicious and scalp the

During nest-building the cock brings material which he passes to the hen who adds it to the nest.

To check the eggs whilst the parent is sitting, carefully lift the bird just sufficiently to expose the eggs.

hen by pecking at the feathers and skin at the top of the head. This will not cause serious injury, but very often the skin is permanently damaged, causing the feathers to grow in an haphazard manner in subsequent years. This occurs more with yearlings than old birds, as the yearlings are boisterous and are unused to the system.

It is also worth noting that it is advisable to let the cock have the same nestbox each year, as the cock is more territorial than the hen and, if given a new nestbox, will always make for the old one and try to reclaim it which can involve quite vicious fighting. Hens are much easier to settle to new nestboxes.

Once all pairs are in the nestboxes, leave them alone for about half an hour. On returning, if it appears that a cock and a hen are not going to pair together, let them out of the loft, and usually, away from the confines of the nestbox and out in the fresh air, they can be seen pairing together on the loft roof when landing. Check the pairs periodically over, say, a couple of hours and, when they appear to have settled down nicely, place a nestbowl in each box, at opposite ends of adjacent nestboxes, so that if a bird goes into the wrong box by mistake it will know the difference.

The next step is to teach the pairs to find their own nestbox, and this is achieved by allowing one pair out at a time, for about half an hour, and letting them find their own way back to their nestbox. This requires a lot of patience, and particularly so with yearlings as they are new to the system. Of course, if they attempt to gain another's box they then have to be caught and placed back in their own.

Once the birds appear fairly comfortable with

the idea of where they should be, let out two pairs at a time, one pair from a top nestbox, the other from a bottom box, so that they will have little difficulty recognizing where they should be. This process should be continued until all the pairs are out at the same time and are trained to return to their boxes. Then and only then should they all be let out of the loft for exercise. When they go back into the loft, care must be taken to ensure that there is no fighting because birds have claimed the wrong boxes.

The excitement of having a nestbox and a mate stimulates the sex glands and soon the cocks start to follow the hen everywhere – this is known as 'driving' and continues until the hen lays the first egg. During the period between driving and laying, the birds should be allowed as much freedom on the outside of the loft as possible, and the cocks spend hours collecting nesting material – twigs, sticks, and so on –

which the hens place in the nestbowls. Straw, placed by the fancier in the loft, is also industriously gathered and used as nesting material.

Colour

The colour, plumage patterns and sex of the pigeon are all in the genes, which are carried in the chromosomes, these being found in the nucleus of the body cells. These chromosomes are in matched pairs and every pigeon has a total of sixty-two pairs of chromosomes – thirty-one pairs from the sire and thirty-one pairs from the dam – carrying a large number of genes, some of which are matched and some single. The chromosomes carrying the genes that determine colour are the 'X' chromosomes; these also determine the sex of the pigeon. The matched genes are called 'allelomorphs' and it must be

These chicks are days old and should only be checked if necessary.

noted that whilst the genes determine character, the allelomorphs (partners) control the form the character will take.

Pigeons belong to two pigmentation groups: ash/red (with wing pattern red, red chequers, or mealies) and black/blue (with wing pattern blue, blue chequers, chequers, or dark chequers). Thus a pigeon having two ash/red determining genes will have ash/red plumage, whilst a pigeon having two black/blue determining genes will have black/blue plumage. If the pigeon has one ash/red and one black/blue gene, it will be ash/red in colour, as this is dominant to black/blue.

Cocks pass colour to both sons and daughters, whilst hens can only pass colour to their sons. So, a black/blue cock mated to an ash/red hen will produce a cock of ash/red colour as this is the dominant gene, however the cock will also have the black/blue colour genes which are hidden, so will be able to pass on to his offspring either the ash/red or the black/blue colour. An ash/red hen cannot produce black/blue cocks. If the aforementioned parents produce a hen, however, it will be of black/blue colour as a hen can only inherit colour from her sire.

The wing pattern is passed from both parents to both cocks and hens, so a red chequer hen mated to a red cock could produce both red and red chequer cocks and hens, and this in turn is the only pattern which they can pass on to their progeny.

The Egg

When the sperm of the cock fuses with the ovum of the hen, the first cell of the new youngster is

Newly hatched youngster in the nest.

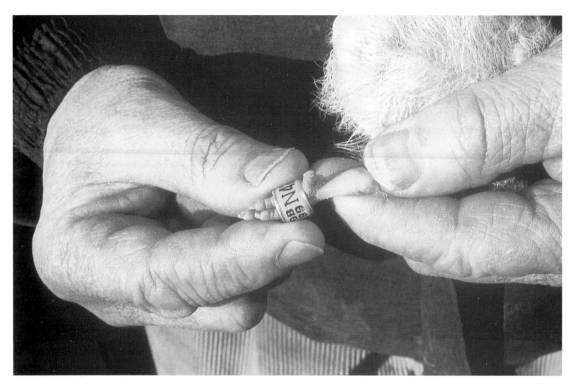

Ringing the youngster at eight days of age.

formed, which then divides to form two identical cells. These further divide, becoming four and then eight and so on until there is a mass of cells all containing sex, size, colour and body formation, inherited in equal parts from the parent. The first egg is laid around eight days after pairing, followed by the second egg about two days later, and then the parents begin 'sitting'. The hen usually has the 'night shift' – evening until the following morning – and then the cock will sit from morning until evening; the bird which is sitting will continue until relieved by its mate. At about nine days it can be ascertained which eggs are fertile and which infertile as the fertile eggs become opaque and those infertile remain clear. Meanwhile, around the tenth day of sitting, the formation of the soft food with which the young will be fed for the first seven to nine days has commenced in the parents.

Providing the environment and warmth from the sitting parent is maintained, a good quality youngster will be hatched. The embryo develops until the seventeenth or eighteenth day, and about twenty-four hours before hatching the embryo is complete, except that what is left of the yolk sac is outside the abdomen of the embryo which is still breathing by means of the egg membrane and porous eggshell. As the blood supply to the eggshell membrane gradually lessens, the means of the embryo to obtain oxygen and give off carbon dioxide becomes diminished and it is thought that, as the embryo begins to struggle to breathe, this movement causes the egg yolk sac to be drawn into the abdomen. The head turns and the egg tooth, which is on top of the beak, rips the now dry and brittle eggshell membrane, the shell gives way to the pressure from within and the youngster breaks out.

There will be occasions when the youngster reaches this stage of development but is then unable to break out of the shell. After some time it becomes exhausted and dies in the shell. This condition is referred to as 'dead in shell'. The cause of such death is not fully understood and is either an inherited weakness in the youngster, or the shell is too strong due to the hen having excess calcium in the blood. One or two deaths from this cause per breeding season is to be expected, but if it becomes a problem expert help should be sought.

The Youngster

The newly hatched youngster, or nestling, can seem very vulnerable to the novice fancier as it gives an appearance of utter helplessness but, in fact, all it needs at this moment in time is to be kept warm. The remains of the yolk sac which has been drawn into its abdomen gives it the necessary nourishment for the first twenty-four hours of its life, and on the second day it starts to take the soft food produced by both parents who take turns to feed it; like all new-born, as each day passes it takes in bigger quantities.

An interesting feature of the nestling's early development is the rapid growth of the digestive organs, and it is noticeable that they do not defecate for the first few days. This is because the soft food is completely digestible so there is no waste matter to excrete. The rapid development of the digestive organs prepares the nestling for handling large amounts of solid food as soon as possible. In the short space of

Young pigeons, about fourteen days old, in the nest.

three weeks, the nestling will have to grow a complete set of feathers and bone, muscle and nerves, so the digestive organs have to be sufficiently developed to cope with the task of extracting nutrients from the food for this purpose.

At only a few days old there is a darkening of colour and the pin feathers can be seen growing in the follicles. By the age of seven or eight days the youngster must be 'rung' using the rings obtained from the Union or Association (*see* Chapter 6). If they are rung before this age the ring can easily slip off the leg and become lost, so it is important that ringing is carried out at the correct time. The opposite could also occur and the pigeon's leg become too thick to take the ring; if this happens, the youngster cannot be raced in the future. The ring is usually placed upside down on the right leg so that the fancier, when handling the bird, can read the number. The three front toes, which point forwards, must be put through the ring first and then the ring pulled over the pad, the back toe and claw until it is possible to pull the back toe through the ring.

Once the birds have been rung it is necessary to examine them daily for about a week to check that the ring has not fallen off in the nest. Care should be taken when checking the development of both egg and young nestlings. The parent bird will not readily come off the young and can damage them if there is a struggle between fancier and bird to remove the parent from the nest. The fancier should gently slide his hand, palm downwards, under the parent and then carefully lift it from the nest. Often it

When putting the pairs together, take care that the cock does not become too aggressive. This three-year-old hen still carries the damage inflicted to the top of her head after being 'scalped' by her cock on their first pairing.

The newly hatched youngsters should only be examined if necessary. The hatching will be announced when the parent birds remove the egg shells from the nest. Note the perfect cylindrical cut made by the egg tooth of the youngster in order to escape from the shell.

will not be necessary to completely remove the parent as a quick check of the eggs or youngsters is all that is required.

At this time solid food has been introduced to sustain growth and feathering because the youngster has to maintain its own body warmth as the parents spend more time away from the nest. The feathers appear at about ten days and the cock will shortly start to drive the hen to nest again. It will be noticed that between twelve to eighteen days old the 'squeaker' – so named

because of the noise it makes when hungry – seems to have a large abdomen with patches having no feathers. If inspected carefully it will be noticed that the gizzard is in constant motion as it grinds the food in the first stages of digestion. The youngster's diet has now changed to corn, water and grit fed by the parents, so it is very important that the parent birds have plenty of each in front of them at all times during this stage.

When the squeakers are about sixteen or

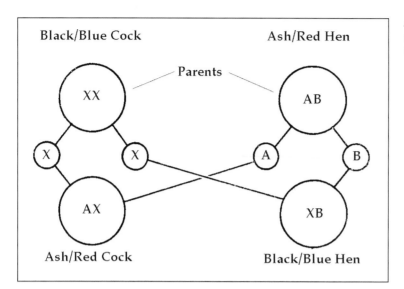

Black/Blue Cock Ash/Red Hen

Parents

XX AB

X X A B

AX XB

Ash/Red Cock Black/Blue Hen

A diagram showing what happens when a black/blue cock is mated to an ash/red hen.

seventeen days old, the hen usually lays again and now the majority of the feeding is undertaken by the cock. If it is not intended to rear more youngsters the newly laid eggs should be removed and substituted by artificial eggs. Three or four days after the original eggs should have hatched, the birds will leave the eggs and prepare to go to nest again. The hen lays approximately every thirty-five days if the eggs are allowed to hatch and approximately every thirty-one days if this is prevented.

Weaning

When the youngsters are nicely feathered under the wing, usually at about twenty-one days old, they can be weaned. They should be taken away from their parents and placed in a separate compartment which is to be their home for the rest of the season. They should be examined individually at this time and any weaklings should be suppressed. For the first two weeks corn should be in front of the youngsters all the time, but the main consideration is that they should drink, so fresh water should also be available at all times. This should be changed daily and for the first couple

of days each youngster should be carefully picked up and their beak inserted into the water trough. Many of the young will not have drunk since being weaned and it is most rewarding to feel a young bird take its first gulp of fresh, clean water.

The youngsters will very soon begin to fly up to the perches, and as their wing and tail feathers become stronger they begin to get more adventurous. Their wattles turn white, their feathers tighten up and they begin to look like racing pigeons. At this time it is as well to inspect them again and make selections. The well-reared youngster can be distinguished by sight and handling. They should be firm and buoyant in the hand, and the neck feathers should gleam and be tight of feather like the old birds. However, some of the bigger built pigeons do take longer to develop so allowance must be made for these. At six weeks old youngsters start to go through a period of 'survival of the fittest'. They are becoming very inquisitive and this is the period when their muscles are developing. Many youngsters left the nest with straight keels but now develop a twist in the keel because the keel has not hardened from cartilage to bone and, if undue stress is placed on the pectoral muscles on one side of the body, the anchor (the keel) can be affected. Feeding can have an effect on the rate at which the bone hardens, and crooked keels are more common among the bigger built birds as it takes longer for their bones to harden.

Always remember that a youngster is as much a product of its environment (food, hygiene, management) as its heredity, and both share an equal part in that youngster's formation. The environment is down to the fancier; a good environment gives the hereditary factors every chance, a bad environment will ruin that chance. Above all, the environment must be constant to allow for consistent success.

6 ORGANIZATION OF RACES

Organizations

The basic unit of nearly every pigeon racing organization is the local club. These clubs are the backbone of the sport and the majority of racing is conducted here. However, like any competitive activity, there are occasions when the participants disagree and somebody has to act as referee. This is why there are rules to govern the activities and conduct of the members. In the early days of the sport clubs were organized into 'unions' and even today many still maintain the word 'union' in their title.

The principal pigeon association within the United Kingdom is the Royal Pigeon Racing

Three popular clocks: the Benzing (right) and the S.T.B. (left) both print the time on the paper roll within the clock; the Toulet puncture is in the centre.

The clock is open, showing the print roll.

Association (RPRA). This organization was started in 1897 and was known as the National Homing Union. Later it became the Royal National Homing Union until the name was finally changed to its present title. At about the same time, just prior to the beginning of the twentieth century, other associations came into being, specifically related to their geographical positions, for example The Scottish Homing Union, The Welsh Homing Pigeon Union, The Irish Homing Union and The North of England Homing Union. These are the major organizations within the UK, but the RPRA is by far the largest with a membership of over 50,000.

At grass-roots level the clubs are grouped into federations, which usually have their own transporters to provide a race service for their member clubs. Transporters are purpose-built lorries, some rigid, some articulated, which are designed to carry birds to the racepoint and effect their simultaneous release. The load-carrying part of the vehicle is constructed with racking which allows the individual race panniers, or crates, to be loaded on to the vehicle from the side. Metal troughs are built into the sides of the racks and these are filled with water and food when the vehicle reaches the racepoint. Each crate, or pannier, is designed with an opening door at one end and this door is attached to the opening mechanism of the transporter. When the lever on the transporter is pulled, all the crate doors open and the pigeons are released.

Often several federations will join together for

transportation and share the costs. Such groups are known as 'combines' or 'amalgamations'. Clubs which are members of federations have their own prize system but members can also compete for prizes within the federation to which they belong. Each club has its own, clearly defined geographical area, which is incorporated into the rules of the club and is referred to as the club's radius. This may be a circle of fixed radius drawn on a map, but can also be defined by reference to several fixed points enclosing an area. All members' lofts must be within the fixed radius and if a member moves to a new address outside the radius his membership is terminated.

The club is administered by rules laid down by the association or union to which it is affiliated with a few domestic rules peculiar to that club. None of the domestic rules may conflict with the general rules of the Association, however. The club is obliged to hold an annual general meeting when officials are elected. A typical club would be expected to have a president or chairman, a treasurer, a secretary and auditor plus several committees, for example a clock committee, a basketing committee and an emergency committee, each dealing with its own specific function within the club.

The Royal Pigeon Racing Association covers the whole of Great Britain and Ireland and for administrative purposes this area is divided into thirteen regions. Each region is autonomous, with its own rules governing its own activities, though again none of these rules may conflict with the main Association rules. Each club is therefore affiliated to its own local region and may be represented at regional level by club delegates elected at the club annual general

A Toulet clock dial showing punctures in the minute dial.

meeting, the number of delegates dependent on the number of members. The local regions elect their own committee from the club delegates and appoint officers such as president, secretary and treasurer. Disputes between club members are dealt with, in the first instance, by the club concerned, and there are specific rules laid down to cover the conduct of disputes. Either party to the dispute can appeal to their local region against their club's decision and the regional committee will re-hear the case from both parties. Following adjudication on the matter, either party again has a further avenue of appeal to the full Council of the Association.

The Council of the RPRA is the sport's principal governing body and consists of delegates from the thirteen local regions. Each region can appoint one, two or three delegates depending on the number of members in the region. At present there are thirty Council members but this can fluctuate according to the membership of the regions. The principle function of the Association is the supply of rings to members, the maintenance of a central ring registry, calculation of flying distances, allocation of race liberation sites, organization of races – especially those from overseas racepoints – plus many ancillary tasks associated with the sport. Each January the Association sends out about 800,000 rings to members. The headquarters of the Association is at Cheltenham where the Council maintains a fully staffed office with a general manager in charge.

In addition to the above, the Association produces and publishes its own weekly and monthly magazines, where both authors of this book work full-time. Magazine production is carried out at offices at Welshpool in

Race rubbers – the rubber is placed on the bird's leg; the counterfoil goes into the clock envelope.

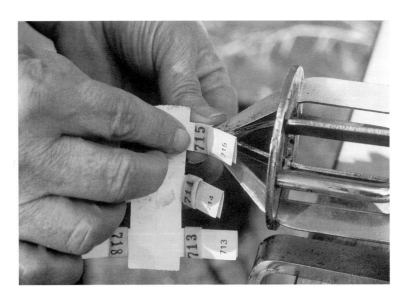

A race rubber being placed on to the ringer.

Mid-Wales and the weekly *British Homing World* is sold world-wide to both members and non-members of the Association.

Although the above information is unique to the RPRA, similar provisions exist within the other Associations and Unions mentioned. Pigeon racing is currently big business, and the Royal Pigeon Racing Association has a staff of approximately forty, ownership of two valuable properties and an annual turnover of over £500,000.

Race Results

It is often assumed by people outside the sport of pigeon racing that the result of the race is determined by the fancier recording the bird's arrival time with a stopwatch. 'Don't some cheat by giving the wrong time?' is a frequent question. In fact the opposite is true. This sport is one of the cleanest, with such tight rules and regulations that it is almost impossible to cheat on the time, as the bird's arrival is recorded by the use of complicated timing clocks. Race results are compiled by computer from exact distances between liberation site and fancier's loft, measured to the yard. The time of flight is

recorded to the second, the winning bird being the bird with the highest velocity (speed), shown as yards travelled per minute (often abbreviated to 'ypm').

In theory, it is possible to arrive at a completely accurate result, but there are a number of imponderables that certainly affect the race and give rise to many hours of heated debate between fanciers. Race results are based on the assumption that the birds leave the transporting vehicle simultaneously. In reality this does not happen; some birds show a reluctance to leave the vehicle and, when they are airborne, nature dictates that they will circle for several minutes before striking off for home. This time wasted at the racepoint varies according to the weather and experience of the pigeons involved and, especially in short, fast races, will affect the result. The calculations also assume that the birds travel from racepoint to home loft in a straight line but again this is not the case. Variable wind conditions will cause the bird to deviate from left to right of a straight line and even fly in a zig-zag pattern.

A feature known as the 'drag' also comes into play. Pigeons are gregarious by nature and prefer the company of other pigeons during flight. The tendency is to stay with the group for as long as possible, and it is only the champion bird that is able to shake off this natural inhibition and make its way home alone. In many races the birds remain in large groups from the liberation point until they are only ten or fifteen miles from home. The groups then begin to break up and head for their individual lofts. Fanciers whose lofts are on the fringe of the area of the club can be adversely affected by the 'pull' of the majority of the club's birds, and this is the feature known as the 'drag'. However, the above mentioned fanciers will not always be at a disadvantage as there will be occasions when a strong cross-wind will push the majority of the birds towards that fancier's location, giving him the chance to reap his rewards.

The problems outlined above have a far greater influence on shorter races than on a race over several hundred miles. In the longer races such imponderables have less effect than the general fitness of the birds which becomes the principal factor that separates the winners from the losers. A further inequality is the different distances that the birds fly to their home loft. In a small club there will only be a distance of a few miles between the lofts of the longest and shortest flying members, but this distance can be much greater in larger clubs and federations. There are also the specialist clubs which only stage a few races each year, but their area is often vast, with hundreds of miles between the lofts of the longest and shortest flying members. An athlete can only maintain his top speed for a short time; compare the world record speed for 100 metres with that of 1,500 metres and it is obvious that the longer the race, the slower the average speed. In pigeon racing all the birds start at the same point but travel different distances and it is impossible to compensate for this inequality. For this reason, in the large specialist clubs the area is divided into sections so that members compete against each other in their own section and also against the whole area in the 'open' result. In many respects these are races within races, and, in a similar manner, local club members compete against members of other clubs within their federation.

Calculating the Race Result

Before being able to calculate the winner of a race it is necessary to know the exact distance between racepoint and loft and an accurate time between liberation and arrival. The distance is calculated in miles and yards from a loft location 'pricked' on a map of the area to a similar

The race rubber is placed on the bird's leg. The ringer expands the race rubber to allow it to pass over the foot.

pinprick showing the location of the racepoint. Shortly after being admitted as a member of a club, the new fancier will be visited by club officials who will make a pinprick in the club map at the location of their loft. The club map is a large-scale Ordnance Survey map and this is then forwarded to a central office for calculation of the loft's longitude and latitude. This co-ordinate is given as degrees, hours, minutes and seconds. A typical example would be shown as:

| Latitude | 52 | 47 | 21.69 | North |
| Longitude | 3 | 4 | 29.08 | West |

A latitude shown as 'north' means that it is north of the equator, whilst a 'west' longitude shows that the loft is west of the 0° line of longitude known as the Greenwich meridian. Whilst all UK lofts will have a northern latitude, longitudes can be either east or west of the Greenwich meridian.

The central office (RPRA headquarters in most cases) holds all the different co-ordinates of the various racepoints, and liberations can only take place from these authorized sites. A computer programme at the headquarters calculates the exact distance from each racepoint to each fanciers' loft and the club is supplied with member's distances for all the racepoints used by the club, with a copy supplied to the member. This shows the racepoint, the racepoint code number, the distance in miles and yards and then the same distance in sixtieths of a yard. This latter distance is necessary when calculation of the velocity is made as the two vital pieces of information are the flying time in seconds and the distance in sixtieths of a yard. The resulting answer will then be given as a speed, or velocity, in yards per minute, for example:

$$\text{Velocity} = \frac{\text{distance (in 60ths of a yard)}}{\text{flying time (in seconds).}}$$

This final calculation is taken to three decimal places which ensures that the chance of a 'dead

heat' is remote. However, many fanciers are of the opinion that when a result is closer than one yard per minute the result *should* be given as a dead heat.

The only other imponderable to affect the result of a race is the variation of the clock; that is, where a clock is fast or slow at the time of recording the arrival of the bird. With modern clocks using a quartz movement such variation is very little, often only one or two seconds, but with the older mechanical clocks the variation can be several minutes. Such a wide variation is undesirable, as any calculation assumes that the clock varies at a constant rate from when set before the race to timing the bird. If this rate of variation is not constant an inaccurate result can occur.

For the calculation of a race result, four distinct times are required:

(1) the time at which the clocks are set or 'struck' (usually on the night before the race)
(2) the time at which the birds are liberated
(3) the time at which the bird arrives home
(4) the time at which the clocks are checked after the race.

Using these four times it is possible to work out how fast or slow the clock was at the time the bird arrived. If a clock is set at 8.00pm on Friday night and checked at 8.00pm on Saturday, this total run of the clock is called the 'long run', and over a period of twenty-four hours it is quite easy to tell if the clock has gained or lost and by how many seconds. This gain or loss is known as the 'total variation'. What then needs to be established is the proportion of this total variation that applied at the time the bird arrived. The period from the time that the clock was set to the time of arrival of the bird is known as the 'short run' and when this is shown as a fraction of the total variation it gives the variation applicable at the time of the bird's arrival, for example:

$$\text{Actual Variation} = \frac{\text{short run x total variation}}{\text{long run.}}$$

This actual variation is then either subtracted from or added to the time of the bird's arrival to establish the exact time that the bird arrived.

This explanation may seem complicated, but with the use of modern computers for the calculation of race results only the basic information has to be fed into the computer for an accurate result to be obtained. The excitement at club headquarters on race night whilst all this information is being put into the club's computer is intense. Approximate times of member's arrivals are known but it is only after all the data has been fed into the computer that the result can be printed out, usually with a copy supplied to each club member.

Timing Clocks

With such precise results it is essential that special clocks are used. The arrival of the bird at the home loft is recorded by taking a special race rubber (*see* page 94) from the leg of the pigeon, placing this into a thimble and inserting it into an aperture in the clock. The clock is then 'struck' by pressing a lever, or handle, which moves the internal mechanism, taking the thimble with the race rubber into the clock where it cannot be retrieved until the clock is opened later by race officials. The same action

records the time, either by a puncture through dials, a print on to a roll of paper, or an entry into the clock's built-in computer chip. As the numbers on the race rubbers are recorded at the time the bird was race marked, this not only confirms that a bird arrived at the time shown but also the identity of the particular bird.

Over the years, a number of these specialized clocks have been developed and to follow is a brief description of the four main types: mechanical clocks, quartz clocks, electronic clocks and tagging systems.

Mechanical Clocks

Many types of mechanical clock have been in use since the beginning of the sport in the late 1800s. The movement is traditional clockwork and a record is made by a puncture into a dial. Later mechanical clocks recorded the time by printing on to a paper roll. A typical example is the Toulet clock which has been in existence, with little modification, since the 1920s. These are no longer manufactured, but there are still plenty in regular use. They can take up to fourteen thimbles and the needle strikes upwards through two paper dials, one showing hours and the other minutes and seconds.

The rubber is released and contracts on to the bird's foot.

Quartz Clocks

With the development of quartz timing mechanisms these clocks became popular and are basically the original printer clocks, with the added advantage of a more accurate quartz movement replacing the original mechanics. The STB and Benzing quartz clocks are typical examples and are still popular with many fanciers.

Electronic Clocks

These clocks record the time via an electronic record made into the clock's internal electronic chip, and this information is retrieved at clock checking when it is transferred to a data printer which is supplied with the clock. Only one printer is required, irrespective of how many clocks are used, and if all club members were to use the same type of clock, one data printer would output the full result.

Tagging Systems

There are several of these now on the market, but at the time of writing they are not permitted for competition use in the UK. This is because they do not use the traditional race rubber and thimble method of timing the bird's arrival, but rely on a 'barcode' which is imprinted into a special ring on the bird's leg. When the bird is race marked the code is read by an electronic device similar to the barcode reader used at supermarket checkouts. This information is recorded by computer and the same equipment is used when the clock is checked after the race. On arrival from the race the time is recorded when the bird passes over a device fitted on to the landing board of the loft. There is no requirement to catch the bird, remove the race rubber, put the rubber into the thimble and strike the clock. In fact, the bird need not even enter the loft and the fancier need not be

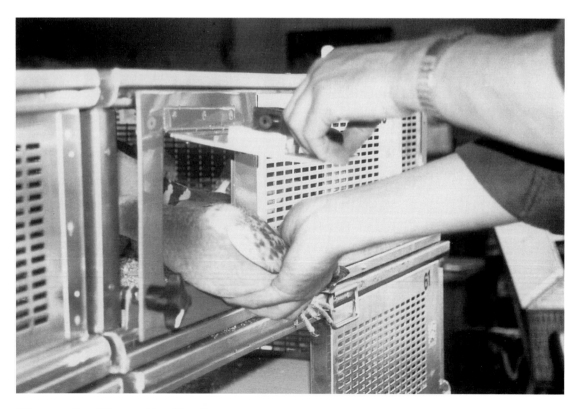

The race-rubbered pigeon is placed into the race pannier.

```
              S & A — SYSTEM 4000 — STRETTON COMPUTERS
              ================================================

         SHREWSBURY TELEPOST H.S.            SAINTES 19/ 7/1998

            20 Members sent 109 Birds.  Liberated at 060000  Wind WSW

Pos   Name              Velocity  Distance Set Chk CorTim  FlyTim   C-S  Ring No   Pools   £££.pp
  1 J. TAYLOR           1541.421 488.1284   0  45 15-18-01 09-18-01  DKC GB96N45592
  2 C. GOUGH            1506.794 488.1447   0  -1 15-30-57 09-30-57  BLC GB95J50818  ABCDE  £17.10
  3 A. HATTON           1492.426 488.1257   0 123 15-36-20 09-36-20  CPH GB96S60424  H      £5.00
  4 W. H. RICHARDS      1476.724 488.0475   0   0 15-41-56 09-41-56  CHC GB96J93523
  5 S. RICHARDS         1475.837 491.0346   0  56 15-45-46 09-45-46  MEC GB95P50550
  6 M. LOVELOCK         1467.857 492.0411   0   1 15-50-12 09-50-12  CHC GB96Z37366  ABCDEF £25.40
  7 A. HATTON           1466.574 488.1257   0 123 15-46-29 09-46-29  CHH GB96S60406
  8 W. H. RICHARDS      1465.976 488.0475   0   0 15-46-12 09-46-12  CHC GB97J95542
  9 A. HATTON           1462.131 488.1257   0 123 15-48-16 09-48-16  BPH GB96S60342
 10 A. HATTON           1461.718 488.1257   0 123 15-48-26 09-48-26  CHC GB96S60402
 11 C & C CHURMS        1461.306 490.1470   0  -3 15-51-09 09-51-09  CHC SU95-400
 12 W. H. RICHARDS      1461.157 488.0475   0   0 15-48-08 09-48-08  BLC GB96J93522
 13 D.S. & J.A. BENNETT 1434.623 490.1322   2  20 16-02-03 10-02-03  CHH GB96S60448
 14 E. WATKINS          1434.551 484.0339   0 255 15-54-02 09-54-02  MEC GB97N49672
 15 S. RICHARDS         1432.129 491.0346   0  56 16-03-39 10-03-39  CHH GB93S74913
 16 MR & MRS J. DOWNES  1427.494 490.1431   0  18 16-05-08 10-05-08  BPH GB95N22627
 17 C & C CHURMS        1424.361 490.1470   0  -3 16-06-29 10-06-29  CHC GB97S67154
 18 E. WATKINS          1413.407 484.0339   0 255 16-02-55 10-02-55  BLC GB95N15756
 19 K. JONES            1379.031 491.0920   0 -22 16-27-18 10-27-18  BLC GB95N23592
 20 B. COOKE            1368.957 480.1240   5 125 16-18-01 10-18-01  CPC GB95C50251
 21 D. JEHU             1351.366 491.0322   0  -7 16-39-42 10-39-42  BLC GB96M10777
 22 P. HARVEY           1336.448 492.0636   0  20 16-48-24 10-48-24  CHH GB97V27012
 23 E. WATKINS          1316.934 484.0339   0 255 16-47-05 10-47-05  CHH GB97N49700


Result printed: Sun 19 Jul 1998 20:14:37
```

A typical printed race result.

present. It is for these reasons that many feel the users of such clocks would have an unfair advantage over members with more traditional clocks. Only time will tell if these clocks gain universal acceptance.

Three-Way Test

At the beginning of each racing season, clocks that are to be used in competition are submitted to the club for an annual three-way test. This is a check to ensure that all clocks run true in different positions. As these positions will vary from clock to clock, full details of how each type of clock is to be tested are contained in the rules of the Association. If they do vary, the variation is constant, irrespective of the position in which the clock is standing. In the past it was discovered that some clocks could gain in one position but lose in another. If a fancier could time his bird into a slow clock and then, simply

RACE SHEET

CLUB *Coventry and District H.S.*

MEMBER'S NAME *Mr and Mrs B. Smith*

DATE.............*14th June 1998*............

RACE POINT.............*Weymouth*............

NUMBER OF BIRDS ...*12*............

RING NUMBERS	COL.	SEX	5	10	25	50	£1	£2	£5			N	INSIDE RUBBER	OUTSIDE RUBBER
GB96 J 31933	blue	hen	X											
GB97 Z 62129	red	cock	X	X	X	X	X	X	X			X		
GB98 N 03023	cheq	cock	X											
GB96 J 31942	blue	hen	X											
GB97 Z 62120	cheq	cock	X											
GB98 N 03033	blue	hen	X											
GB98 N 03025	cheq	cock	X											
GB96 J 31938	red	cock	X											
GB98 N 03035	pied	hen	X											
GB98 N 03043	red	hen	X											
GB97 Z 62133	cheq	cock	X											
GB97 Z 62125	blue	hen	X											

I/we declare that the above birds are my/our property and race to my/our loft.

I/we certify that all the birds listed on this entry form have been vaccinated against paramyxovirus in accordance with current legislation.

signed ....*B. Smith*....................

	BIRDS AT		£	p
12	Race birds at	30p	3	60
12	Birds at	5p		60
1	Birds at	10p		10
1	Birds at	25p		25
1	Birds at	50p		50
1	Birds at	£1	1	00
1	Birds at	£2	2	00
1	Birds at	£5	5	00
1	Nomination at	£1	1	00
	TOTAL TO PAY		14	05

A completed race entry form.

by changing its position, could cause it to gain, he would have a clock that was slow at the time the bird arrived but fast when the clock was checked later. There is only a few seconds advantage, but this could make all the difference in a short, fast race.

The three-way test is usually conducted at club headquarters a few weeks before the first race. Afterwards the clocks are kept in the possession of the club. No fancier is allowed to take his clock home, unless it is locked or sealed for a race, until the end of the racing season. If a clock is inadvertently opened or develops a fault it has to be retested before it can be used again for competition.

The Race

In the United Kingdom the racing season usually begins in April with short races for old birds – birds that have not been bred in the current year – and continues with races gradually increasing in distance until June and July when the longest races are held. By July the old birds are beginning to moult and their racing ceases. Young birds are raced from July until September, when racing finishes for the year. These are the general provisions but there are many exceptions, with some clubs even holding special races on Boxing Day.

The following account is of the events surrounding a typical one-day race, where the birds are race marked on Friday night and the race is held on Saturday.

Having trained the birds to the peak of fitness the fancier makes his team selection for the big day. Generally he enters birds to win, but he may include birds that are being trained for later races and which he feels require the experience of racing in shorter events to prepare them for the longer ones. The details of each entry are

Liberation of a three-vehicle convoy.

At the conclusion of the race, all details are fed into the computer for calculation of the result.

written on a race entry sheet which also records any 'pool' money to be placed on an individual bird. Gambling is not compulsory and many fanciers do not partake in this side of the sport at all, being satisfied with the chance of winning the race and any prize money involved. The race entry fee pays for the cost of transporting the birds to the racepoint with a percentage of this going towards the prize money. Most clubs in this country only race for between three and six prizes, whereas on the Continent the prizes are more widely spread; 25 per cent of entries often receiving prizes. The race entry sheet also contains a declaration from the fancier that entries have been vaccinated against para-myxovirus (*see* Chapter 9). This is a legal requirement before any bird is raced and pro-tects the club secretary in the event of a check on vaccination records.

On arrival at club headquarters the basket of birds and entry form are handed to club marking officials and the fancier is not allowed further contact with his birds. Strict rules prevent any fancier from being involved with the marking of his own birds or the setting of his clock. Birds are removed from the member's basket and 'rung' with one of the special race rubbers that are supplied on a cardboard docket showing the same numbers as the race rubber; for security reasons there is a number on the inside and outside of the docket. The numbers of the race rubbers are recorded on the member's sheet and the rubber is stretched and released on to the leg of the pigeon using a gadget called a 'ringer'. Although the race rubber can easily be pulled off when the bird arrives home it will not come off through normal use and is not tight enough to cause any dis-comfort to the bird.

Once rubbered, cockbirds are placed in

A modern transporter being loaded for the race.

selected panniers and henbirds in others, but not all the pigeons belonging to one fancier go in the same pannier, they are mixed with other fancier's birds. The panniers are then sealed with numbered seals, which are removed just prior to liberation. When all members' birds are in the panniers they are loaded on to the federation transporter. The race entry sheets and cardboard dockets are retained by club officials.

During the time in which the birds are being basketed for a race, the club clock committee will have been busy setting the clocks for competition. Each clock is set to receive a thimble in its first aperture and the date, race, club and name of the clocksetter are endorsed on the roll or dial. Clocks are struck against a special clock called the 'master timer' and details of any variation, fast or slow, are recorded in a clock book. Some clocks have to be sealed using numbered seals similar to those

used on the race panniers, whilst some automatically lock themselves when the setting strike is made. After sealing, the clocks are checked and handed to the competitor.

Meanwhile, the race birds have been collected from club headquarters in the federation transporter. The 'convoyer' is the name given to the federation official in charge and he is responsible for the welfare and safe liberation of the birds. All convoyers are licensed by the local region of the RPRA and a Code of Conduct is published to govern their responsibilities and duties. When all birds have been collected from the various clubs the transporter sets off for the racepoint, the main part of the journey being during the night. On arrival at the liberation site the birds are rested and given access to water.

Race day comes and fanciers anxiously check weather forecasts and scan the sky for other pigeons making their way home. From watching other pigeons flying over, an experienced eye can gauge their speed which will give the fancier an indication of the speed that can be expected from his own race birds. At the liberation site the convoyer has to be up and about early. He checks his charges to ensure that they have all had access to water and prepares the vehicle for release. He also contacts his race controller at the home-end and discusses the weather and possible problems the birds may encounter. By telephoning his contacts en route, the race controller has established a 'line of flight' report on weather conditions and this is passed on to the convoyer. The race controller also liaises with other race controllers in different areas of the country whose convoys might be criss-crossing his line of flight and, weather permitting, they agree on liberation times which will avoid the convoys clashing on the home flight. After final consultation between convoyer and race controller, all contingencies have been covered to the best of their ability and the birds are released for their journey home.

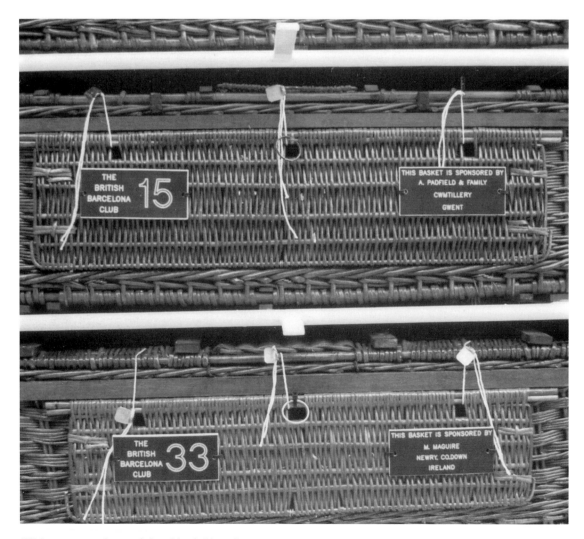

Wicker race panniers, sealed and loaded into the transporter.

Internal view of a modern transporter with central corridor, panniers and drinking troughs.

Each Saturday during the racing season thousands of pigeons take part in numerous races from all parts of the UK and their paths crisscross in every possible direction. How pigeons navigate the course to their home lofts is a constant source of amazement, even to the most experienced fancier.

In due course the fancier hears the information he has been waiting for: 'Birds liberated at 10.00 hours in a south-west wind.' This is either received via a telephone call from the club secretary or from the 'Lib-Line' telephone information service provided by *British Homing World*. The waiting begins, but it is possible to make a calculated guess at the time of arrival, as the wind direction and distance from the race-point are known. On a perfect flying day, with no wind, pigeons will travel at about forty-five miles per hour and, using this as a benchmark, the fancier can estimate how fast his birds will travel and when they can be expected. As time presses on excitement grows and every passing crow, blackbird or woodpigeon is considered a possible first bird, before the vigil is rewarded and a race bird swoops for the loft. Great patience is needed, especially if the bird appears excited or unwilling to enter the loft. Time is ticking away but the fancier knows that any attempt to rush the bird could startle it into the air for a few extra laps before it again settles on the trap. After what seems an age, but is probably only a matter of seconds, the bird enters the loft and the fancier hurries to catch the bird and remove the race rubber from its leg. The fancier must be conscious that any rough handling might make the pigeon even more reluctant to enter the loft in subsequent races, and many a good racer has been made into a bad trapper by thoughtless actions on the part of the owner.

The race rubber is carefully removed from the bird's leg, put into the thimble and then into the clock. The clock is now struck and this records the time of the bird's arrival. In some races a fancier will only time one bird, but there will be occasions when quite a number of birds are timed. In a hard race, when it is expected that there will be quite a time difference between the leading birds, it is safer to time-in several birds as these may figure in the prize list. Also, at the time of clocking the birds the fancier has no idea of the finishing times of any of the birds belonging to his fellow competitors, so it is better to be safe than sorry.

Most clubs require a verification card to be completed by the fancier which shows the numbers of birds that the fancier has clocked, the times and the pools in which they are entered. This assists the secretary when reading the clocks and is also a further security measure. The clocks are returned to the club for checking at a designated time on the night of the race. They are again 'struck' against the master timer and details on the clock seals are checked to ensure that the clock has not been tampered with after leaving the clubhouse on the night of marking the birds. It is not until the clocks are opened that the thimbles containing the race rubbers can be retrieved and checked against the details on the race entry sheet. If the numbers do not correspond the bird is disqualified and there have been occasions when a bird, missing from the previous week's race, is timed-in by mistake, much to the embarrassment of the owner.

Times taken from the clocks are input into the club computer and eventually the last entry is made. This is the moment that everyone has been waiting for: the race result is printed out and copies are handed to each member. Some are elated, others disappointed, but there is plenty of friendly banter and after handshakes all round, members make their way home already planning their strategy for success in the next race.

7 TRAINING AND RACING YOUNG BIRDS

The Young Bird Programme

Every activity around the loft should be geared towards preparation for the days when the birds are competing in races. If the pigeons are allowed to develop bad habits as youngsters these will continue when they are racing. The greatest frustration for the pigeon fancier is the bird that arrives home from the race and sits out on the loft, ignoring all efforts by the fancier to persuade it to enter and be timed-in. Such behaviour is the result of either bad habits learned as a youngster or of being handled roughly when arriving home from previous races.

Training of young birds begins from the day they are weaned from their parents. When the young birds are first weaned it is better to have food in front of them during all daylight hours, but as soon as it is seen that the birds are picking up their food with confidence, this practice should be replaced by a two meals per day routine; one feed in the morning and one in the evening. At this stage the fancier should begin to train the birds to come in for their food at his call or whistle. Young birds quickly learn the sound of the fancier's voice and respond to this, knowing that when they hear that call it will be time to eat.

The fancier should always be aware of the presence of the birds when he is moving around the loft. Sudden movements and bangs will startle the birds and this is not what is wanted. The birds should have enough confidence to almost ignore the fancier when he is working or moving about the loft, and as soon as he calls them for food they should come running. It

takes practice before this is achieved and there is a fine balance between giving the birds sufficient food for them to develop properly, and restricting their food in order to maintain discipline. Unfortunately, the food supply is the only means of keeping young pigeons under control and it takes a degree of trial and error before the correct balance can be maintained. After a few days of the two-meals-per-day routine, the young birds will quickly respond to the fancier's call at food time, and only when this has been achieved is it time to progress to the next stage.

Before the young birds can actually fly it is beneficial to get them outside the loft to enable them to have a look at their surroundings. It is during these early days that the birds 'log' the exact position of the loft into their brains and it is these early lessons that they will rely on in the years to come. No-one really knows how a racing pigeon finds its way home from a site possibly hundreds of miles away, but current thinking is that there are a number of different factors that need to be taken into account. Generally speaking, the pigeon uses several different instincts to reach its home loft, but these 'built-in' homing instincts only bring it to within five to ten miles of home. It then relies on memory and eyesight to find its own individual loft within this small radius. Bearing this in mind, it is important that the young birds quickly learn the location of the loft in relation to the surrounding countryside. If they are allowed to look out from an early age they will have developed some of this knowledge before they can actually fly and get into difficulties away from the loft.

At this stage the young birds should never

be let out unattended. There is always a danger from predators, either hawks or falcons striking from the air, or cats on the ground. If a predator strikes, the birds will be panicked into premature flight and be scattered all over the adjoining area, often in locations where they cannot be found and retrieved. At this age the birds will be reluctant to leave the safety of the loft and will constantly attempt to get back in. It is during these early weeks that the sputnik trap is most useful. The young birds may be lifted and placed in the trap and left there for a few hours before they can actually fly. This gives them the advantage of being able to see out of the loft and view their surroundings without the danger of being startled by predators. Fanciers without such traps often construct a small cage from wire mesh and place this on the landing board of the loft. The youngsters can then be

placed in the cage and left for several hours in perfect safety.

The First Flight
When the youngsters are first weaned from their parents they will be confined to the floor of the loft as they are unable to fly, but after a week or so they will begin to fly up to the perches to roost at night. They are then ready to be given their first taste of freedom. Rather than force the birds out of the loft it is better to open the trap or door and leave them to it. Young pigeons have a natural curiosity and, after they have gained confidence, they will emerge and fly up on to the roof of the loft. The birds should be given this type of freedom for about one hour every day, and when this time is up they should be called into the loft for their feed. It makes no difference whether this is done in the morning

A wire pen constructed to protect young pigeons as they become accustomed to their surroundings.

or evening, but it is essential that they learn to come in immediately the fancier calls and are rewarded with food. Whilst the birds are still at this stage in their development they should also be schooled to enter the loft through the trap or bobwires, or whatever trapping device is to be used during the races. Young birds are the most stubborn of creatures and it is often a battle of wills between pigeon and fancier to get the bird to enter the loft by the correct entrance when called. Here again the only encouragement is food, and great patience is needed by the fancier to train his birds in this elementary requirement for quick trapping following the races.

After about two weeks of this type of training the young pigeons will be confident in going out of the loft, sitting on the roof and entering through the trap when the fancier calls. At some point they will decide for themselves that it is

time to take to the air and will undertake their first venture into the unknown. It is fascinating to watch young birds making their first attempts at flight. They are clumsy and awkward, but after the first one has made its maiden voyage it is not long before the remainder of them pluck up the courage to follow suit. What a sight it makes when twenty or thirty young pigeons first take to the air. They veer and swerve in erratic flight patterns, often colliding with each other, eventually coming to land on the loft or any other suitable building in the area. Once they have landed after their initial flight, they will need some time to regain their depleted energy and confidence to make a second flight. This is not a problem as this stage only lasts for a few days and soon the group will begin to fly together in close formation, getting bolder and bolder as they begin to explore the area

Youngsters should be trained to be confident in the basket. Here the basket has been placed on the loft landing board. Note the water trough.

surrounding their home loft. Again, this is all part of an essential learning pattern, but the fancier must ensure that the birds continue to observe all the previous lessons as well: food twice a day; entering the loft via the trap; coming into the loft when called.

Sometimes a minor noise or event will cause the youngsters to make their first flight – a car backfiring in the street or a neighbour's washing suddenly billowing in the wind. This startles the birds into flight and, once they have taken this first step, they are always keen to take to the air on release from the loft. There will be occasions, however, when birds reach the stage of going out of the loft and on to the roof but do not appear to want to progress further. Some think that this indicates lazy birds, but more often than not it is because they have not been prompted into flight by some unusual noise. If the fancier feels that it is time the birds were flying but they show no inclination, the simple remedy is to provide the stimulus. Throwing an object a few feet into the air is usually sufficient, but care should be taken that this is not over-done as the objective is to get the birds to take to the air, not scare them out of their wits.

After a few weeks the team of young birds should be flying well. In ideal circumstances they should be released for exercise twice a day, morning and evening, the length of time depending on the fancier's circumstances, but after each flight they should be called into the loft and given their feed. As the weeks progress they will become more and more confident, sometimes disappearing for ten to fifteen minutes at a time. Although they are out of sight they rarely roam outside a five-mile radius of the loft unless something unexpected happens that causes them to panic. This may be an attack by a predator hawk, the sound of a shotgun, or simply getting mixed up with other groups of pigeons that are travelling from a race or training trip. When the youngsters are at this age, many fanciers do not let their young birds out for exercise at times when older race birds are likely to be passing through the area, for example Saturday race days. Another

dangerous time is Wednesday afternoon when midweek clubs stage their events. A team of young birds at exercise round their loft can be quickly swept away by a race team and may end up many miles from home, completely lost and with insufficient strength to fly home.

Flyaway
Experiences such as those outlined above can be partly to blame for the dreaded 'flyaway', which results in the loss of many young birds. A team of young birds at exercise will disappear and be missing for several hours. Sometimes they return intact, but more often than not only a few of the team return and the others are never seen again. This is very discouraging for the fancier, especially in his early days when he is attempting to build a strong team of racing pigeons. However, the budding fancier must face facts; no matter how carefully he chooses his stock, how well his young birds are bred or how thorough the training, there will always be losses of young birds, and it is at this stage of the training programme that the majority of these losses occur.

Although the actual cause of a flyaway is not known, there are a number of common indicators that may be present when such a disaster occurs. The day might be a good day for flying when the youngsters 'feel their feet' and fly for the sheer fun of it; especially if released early in the morning the birds will be away, flying for all they are worth. Is it any wonder then that they sometimes get out of their depth and, with the exhilaration of the early morning flight, roam much farther than normal. On realizing they are lost, panic sets in, the group break up and many join other groups of pigeons that are in the sky at the same time. If these groups are from another part of the country the lost youngster tags along and ends up far from home, hungry, exhausted and, if he is lucky, in another fancier's loft.

It is felt by many that another of the prime causes of a flyaway is overcrowding in the loft. In nature, a colony of Rock Doves will live and nest on ledges and in crevices of cliffs and, when the colony reaches such numbers that they are no longer sustainable by the available food, a number of the youngsters will fly off to begin a new colony. This is probably what happens in a loft where youngsters have to fight for a perch; as soon as they are old enough, they fly off to start another colony. If this is true, it is essential that the fancier takes care not to overcrowd the loft with too many pigeons in order to avoid a large loss of youngsters before they have even entered a training basket. The golden rule is that the number of birds does not exceed 80 per cent of the available perches, which ensures that there is no nightly squabble for a perch.

A further point is the feeding of the youngsters at what is, for them, one of the most dangerous times in their development. When the young birds reach the stage at which they begin to group together and fly as a team, they are at their most vulnerable and their diet should be adjusted to lower their energy whilst still allowing them sufficient nutrients to develop into healthy adults. An increase in the bean and pea (legume) content of their food will slow the birds down and prevent them venturing off on longer flights away from the loft until their other faculties are more fully developed. It is no different to restricting a sixteen-year-old youth from riding a powerful motorcycle until such time as his riding ability and roadcraft are sufficiently developed for him to handle a more powerful machine.

It is usually from early morning flights that the flyaway occurs. Having rested for the night, the young birds cannot wait to get out of the loft and into the air. They are full of energy and raring to go. Once released they soar into the sky and away. Sometimes they return

Take the basket a short distance from the loft to allow the youngsters a view of their surroundings.

into view several times during the first half hour but then disappear for hours. If the team returns intact the fancier can be satisfied that all his lessons have not been in vain and the birds are of sufficient age and experience to cope with a longer flight, but all too often this is not the case and only part of the team returns. Birds that are reported from such flyaways have often travelled hundreds of miles before they become exhausted and seek refuge in another loft.

What must also be understood is that it is necessary for young birds to experience such long flights even before they are put into the basket for formal training. A flyaway can be a good experience for a racing pigeon and the ones that return have learned a valuable lesson. What the fancier should do is to try to delay this experience until the bird has developed sufficiently to be able to cope with the long flight and the initial panic of being lost and far away from home. It is possible to deter the birds from long flights by restricting them to evening exercise when, because of the advancing twilight, they are reluctant to fly far from the home loft. This is probably a good policy for the first few weeks after the birds begin to fly, but it should not be practised indefinitely as it will only delay the inevitable and birds with little or no experience will be put into the training basket before they have gained sufficient experience of flying in the locality of their home loft.

Basket Training

A regular topic of debate between fanciers is the question of when the formal training of young birds should commence and how much experience the birds should have before the first race. We have always felt that the more training the better, but there is a danger that overtrained young birds get bored by the constant routine of regular training in the basket and merely come home from a race rather than racing home to win. Like nearly everything in pigeon racing, it is a question of getting the right balance and it is only with experience that the fancier learns to read the signs that the birds need more, or less, training. Young birds have a boundless source

of energy and it is difficult to overtrain them, but there are instances of fanciers who basket train their youngsters two or even three times a day, which can lead to them being overtrained. This is also demanding on the time and pocket of the fancier. Pigeon racing is a sport and it should never be allowed to become a burden, either financially or timewise. A good team of young birds which are exercising well morning and evening around the loft do not need more than two or three trips in the training basket every week.

The point at which the birds will be ready for their first basket training is determined by the age of the birds and the experience that they have gained so far. The average fancier will have paired his old birds in mid-February and the youngsters that have been bred should be ready for training by the middle of June. This is about the right time, as the first of the young bird races will be held in late July.

It is a frightening experience for a young bird to be put into a training basket and taken by car for the first training flight. Pigeons do not congregate naturally in such close proximity to each other, and to force them to stand shoulder to shoulder in a confined space can cause them distress. They will fight and peck each other and, when first put into the basket, they will try to escape through the openings. Of course, these openings are only wide enough for them to get their heads and necks through, but the inexperienced pigeons will always try until they realize that escape is impossible. It is not a good idea to put young birds straight into a training basket and take them for their first training flight. It is far better to 'school' them to the basket well before any training flights take place. It is good practice when putting birds into the basket for the first time to leave them in it overnight. It is also a good idea to leave the basket open in the loft for a few days so that the young birds can enter the basket and explore; when it actually comes to putting them into the basket with the lid fastened they are far more confident and quickly settle in the confined space.

Earlier in the chapter it was said to be beneficial to allow the young birds outside the loft before they can fly, and a training basket placed on the landing board is an ideal 'cage' for this purpose. The birds can have a look round outside the loft and at the same time learn that there is nothing to fear from being put into the basket. Basket training is an essential part of a youngster's education as not only does the bird have to gain the confidence of being in the basket, it must also learn to feed and drink in there. The crates used for racing are equipped with drinking troughs which clip on to the outside, allowing the birds to stick their heads out to obtain water. Food supplied for races where the birds spend more than one night in the basket is provided in the empty drinking troughs or by scattering it on the floor of the crate. Young birds need to learn where this food

and water will be available and small troughs can be purchased to clip on to the side of the training basket for this purpose. The youngsters should be left overnight in the basket and fed and watered in this manner so that when they are sent away to races they are fully aware of where their food and water will be available.

The Training Flight

By about the middle of June the average fancier will have his team of young birds ready for their first training flight. They will be experienced in flight away from the loft, fit and healthy enough for several hours of flight, experienced in landing on the loft and coming straight in when the fancier calls, and have knowledge of the confines of the basket so that they do not go into a wild panic when they are caught and basketed. A word of warning here: if any of the above

The first release from the basket should be in the garden, a short distance from the loft.

training stages have not been completed, it is folly to go on to the next stage, as this may well result in an unacceptable number of losses. It is better to wait an extra couple of weeks than miss out on any of the early lessons. Whilst racing young birds is important in order to establish a sound foundation for future racing, it is not essential that all youngsters compete in every race. Some fanciers treat young bird racing as the ultimate accolade and concentrate their efforts on this part of the annual race programme, but the majority look on these races as part of the training process for a future racing career. There are even some fanciers whose young birds do not compete in any races until they are yearlings, but these birds are trained well as young birds without experiencing the trauma of being confined in a race basket overnight.

Every fancier has his own ideas on how to train his young birds, but the majority will start with a training flight over a few miles and gradually increase this to forty or fifty miles. The first 'toss' is the most traumatic for both birds and fancier. Any number of things can go wrong, with the result that a substantial part, or even the whole, of the potential race team never return to the loft. If the steps outlined in this chapter have been followed there is a good chance that such disasters can be avoided, but there is no guarantee, and Mother Nature has scant respect for the hours of work spent by the fancier and can intervene with unpredictable bad weather or hawk attacks.

For the first training toss the fancier should select a day when the weather is fine and clear. The wind should be light, the direction being of little importance at this stage. The middle of the

Applying the wing stamp.

The finished result; any finder can now get in touch with the owner.

morning is the best time, when the predator population should have had their first feed of the day, and there are still plenty of hours of daylight left to allow any birds that split from the main group sufficient time to recalculate their bearings and make for home. It is very rewarding to see a young bird pitch on to the loft late in the evening after being lost all day. Such birds are the ones to cherish for the future.

Five to ten miles is the usual distance for this important first flight and the birds should have been given a light feed of half their normal ration early in the morning but not allowed their usual morning exercise. Care should be taken in catching the birds so as not to frighten them during basketing, and it is always better to catch a pigeon whilst it is stationary on a perch, or the floor of the loft, rather than attempting to catch it in flight. The fancier who rushes the job only brings greater problems on himself as birds that have been roughly captured will be even more reluctant to be caught on a second occasion. All pigeons resent being caught and will avoid the fancier if at all possible, however if the fancier spends time in the loft with the birds they will treat his presence as part of the normal surroundings and will not be alarmed when he tries to catch them. With older birds, it is simple to catch them in their nestboxes. Deep box perches are a blessing in this respect as the bird will retreat into the box rather than attempt to escape by flying out.

The fancier with larger hands has the advantage and the bird is approached by spreading both hands wide with fingers apart to form the largest possible barrier to prevent escape. When both hands are about 18in (45cm) away from the bird and the bird is cowering in the back of the box, slowly move the left hand forward towards the bird. This diverts the bird's attention from the right hand and, whilst the pigeon is watching the left hand approach, quickly slip the right hand over the top of the bird, restraining its flight with downward pressure. The left hand is then slipped under the bird, the legs of the pigeon going between the fancier's fingers with the thumb over the back of the bird to prevent the bird's right wing from moving. The right hand is then turned to form a similar grip on the left side of the pigeon. Held in this manner the bird cannot escape even from the smallest pair of hands, but care should be taken to avoid squeezing the bird too hard as this could easily damage its internal organs. Pigeons never get used to being caught, but the fancier whose birds are tame when in the loft has the least difficulty when trying to catch them. Once caught the bird should be carefully placed in the basket which is then gently put into the car boot.

Care should also be taken in the selection of the liberation site which should be in the general direction from which the birds will eventually race and free from any obstructions that the birds may collide with on release. Overhead wires are a particular problem and it is often difficult to find a suitable spot where these are not in evidence. A large open space such as a car park is ideal, and even though it may not be in the direct line of flight for the races, safety is of greater importance. On arrival at the liberation spot the basket of birds is carefully taken from the car and placed on the ground. It is left there for five to ten minutes to allow the birds to settle and gain their bearings. This resting period is important and recent experiments on the pigeon's homing ability show that birds left to rest for thirty minutes before liberation make their way home immediately after release, whereas birds liberated immediately on arrival at the site tend to circle in the air for much longer before striking off for home.

If young birds are not given this resting period before release on their first flight they are more likely to panic on liberation and make off in any direction before they have had a chance to gain their proper bearings. The fancier has to face the fact that a proportion of the young birds that he has bred will not make successful race birds and will be lost during these early training stages. Many of these are taken by predators but the majority join flocks of feral pigeons and spend the rest of their days happily living in the fields and countryside. Others join groups of pigeons that are passing on similar training flights and end up in the loft of another fancier, but wing stamping and an efficient registration system allow for these lost birds to be returned to their owners in a matter of days. Such pigeons, which have simply made a mistake, have often learned a valuable lesson and, if treated with care, can develop into successful racers. As stated earlier, however, young pigeons are very stubborn and once they have an idea in their heads it is very difficult to remove it. This is often so with young birds that become lost and end up in another fancier's loft; after being returned to their home by public carrier they are released on another training flight only to return to the other fancier's loft. Many fanciers understand this and are quite prepared to transfer ownership of pigeons; these birds often go on to successful racing careers from their 'adopted' loft. Many friendships between fanciers are formed through the loss and transfer of these young birds which often results in the exchange of young birds in subsequent years.

The fancier will return home from the first training flight with a degree of anxiety, hoping that his team will have been able to overcome their fears and have made it home. Don't panic if they take some time to return from this first event. If the earlier training has been completed and the birds are ready, they will come home. However confident a fancier is that everything has been done to help the birds home, it is always a great relief to see them swing into view and alight on the loft from their first training flight. It is of no consequence that they have taken two or three hours to complete what should have been a thirty-minute flight.

The experience of the first flight is then repeated on a daily basis during the weeks before the first young bird race. Patience should be exercised and there should be several releases from the first location before advancing to a longer flight. Once the birds are flying home well and in reasonable time from one spot it is then alright to go on to the next. Again, the distance between these liberations sites should not be too great, only about five to ten miles, with the birds being kept at that location until they return straight home. The important thing is that they are only trained in good visibility and fine weather conditions. Although they will meet with worse conditions during racing it is better not to expose them to additional difficulties during their early training days.

Training of the young birds should be structured so that they have had plenty of experience before the actual race. Training by car should begin about four weeks before the first race, whilst many federations operate some type of training scheme using the federation transporter to train birds during the week. This type of training is invaluable and, if at all possible, the team of young birds should be sent on one or two transporter tosses before the first race. This will gain them experience of being carried in the transporter, and being liberated and flying with pigeons from other lofts. These lofts will all be in a small area so, should any become lost, they will quickly regain their bearings and return home.

The First Race

The distance for the first race will only be between 50 and 100 miles (80–160km), and this will entail race marking on Friday night with a liberation at about 11am on Saturday morning. Although water will be given to the birds before they are released, they will only be fed in the event of a holdover to the next day (Sunday) due to inclement weather. It does not harm the pigeon to go without food for such a short time and it would be detrimental to them if they were expected to make a long flight on a full crop of food. The birds will arrive home at about 2pm on Saturday afternoon and it is best that they had their last feed at about the same time on the Friday. If they are fed just before basketing they are very likely to regurgitate their food when in the basket, and this is not good policy as they will require their food intake to maintain strength for the flight home.

In Chapter 3 we had an in-depth look at feeding for racing and, in this respect, young birds should be treated in a similar manner to the old birds. There are many propriety brands of feed mixtures on the market which have been formulated by experienced fanciers after years of research. It is far better for the less experienced fancier to draw on the knowledge and expertise of others and feed a corn mixture specifically formulated for racing young birds. Nearly all corn merchants will stock such a mixture and it is folly to ignore the benefit of this experience. The birds should have been fed twice daily as previously described and care should be taken to ensure that they have a good ration of food on the Thursday night before the race. This should be followed by a light feed on Friday morning with another light feed at about 2pm. This means that the birds will be starting to get hungry when they return from the race, but will not be so undernourished that, should a longer than anticipated journey take place due to their making a mistake and losing their way, they will be unable to cope.

It is a mistake for an inexperienced fancier to put all his eggs into one basket by sending his entire team of young birds to the first race. Remember, all the birds in the race will be of similar, limited experience, and some fanciers may not have 'schooled' their birds as carefully as others. If only a few of the birds in the convoy panic after release, this fear quickly spreads throughout the convoy and the result can be many empty perches at night. It is often noted that in a difficult race when many birds do not return home before nightfall, some fanciers

For the darkness system the loft is darkened by the use of curtains.

have more birds missing than others. Usually, those who fare better are the fanciers whose teams have had plenty of basket experience before the first race. It is therefore advisable to enter only half your full team so that, should a disastrous first race occur, you still have half the team left to race the following week. Also, if returns from the first race are good it is possible to rest those birds the following week and enter the birds that did not race the first week. The first two races of the young bird season are those in which large losses can occur due to untrained and inexperienced birds being entered, and once these two events have been successfully completed it is safe to enter all the birds that are fit and well every week.

The majority of experienced fanciers consider that a good young bird is one that has flown the young bird programme and only 'nighted out'

on the odd occasion. The fact that it may not have won a prize is of little consequence as that fancier is looking for birds that will develop into reliable racing pigeons for the future.

Every fancier looks forward to the first young bird races as the time when they can put their annual crop of new pigeons to the test. Many will have introduced new birds into their breeding lofts and this is the time when the success or otherwise of new pairings can be assessed. Many weeks of hard work and some expense will have gone into rearing and training these youngsters to get them ready, and care must be taken that nothing is done to hamper their chances in these initial races. The race sheet should be made out in plenty of time, especially if the birds have to be handled before making selections, and this is best done on the night prior to race basketing. On basketing night care should be taken when catching the birds and the fancier should allow plenty of time so that activities are not rushed, as any tension in the body is easily transmitted to the birds. On arrival at the club marking station the birds will be handed over to the marking officials, and following this the fancier feels a sense of helplessness as there is nothing else to be done to ensure the young pigeons make a success of their first race. Whilst basketing is in progress the clocks will be set by the clock committee and members are called on to 'strike' the clock against the master timer kept by the club. No member is allowed to strike his own clock but, once the clock has been checked and its times and variation noted, it is sealed and handed to the owner.

The prudent fancier makes sure that everything is ready for the arrival of the pigeons. Nothing is left to chance: the lofts have been swept out, spare birds put into a separate compartment, and clock and thimbles put out in an easily accessible place. The first bird home is the vital one and it is important that this bird traps quickly. This is all down to training, but when the bird alights on the trap it will hesitate before going inside. If the loft is empty it will be suspicious that all is not well and stay on the trap for a longer period. It is better to leave several pigeons loose within the loft as decoys in order to give the first bird confidence to enter quickly. These birds should be just as hungry as the race birds and not have been fed since the other birds went to the race. They should also be easily distinguishable as it is difficult, when looking from above, to see which bird is carrying a race rubber on its leg. If the decoy birds are of the same colour as the race bird the fancier may have to catch several before selecting the right one. A few grains of corn thrown

Box perches in the young bird loft. Note that there is plenty of space for the inmates.

Young birds are allowed a good look outside the loft before they can actually fly.

on to the floor will keep the decoy birds eating in full view of the bird on the trap who will quickly enter and join in the feeding. It is also easy to catch the bird when its attention is diverted by the food and the fancier can quickly slip his hand over the bird, pick it up and remove the race rubber. Great care must be taken not to frighten young birds as this will have an adverse effect in later races, as a bird startled in the early races will go on to become a bad trapper in later years.

'Trick' Training Methods

So far in this chapter we have only talked about training and racing young birds on a natural system where the birds return because of their natural homing instinct; their only motivation is to be fed and regain their perch before nightfall. For many fanciers this is sufficient motivation as they treat young bird racing as part of their training to race as old birds. In Chapter 8 it is revealed that there are many tricks designed to make the birds come home faster than their competitors. These involve the use of the pigeon's love for his partner and eggs, or his sexual drive to mate and produce offspring. It is possible to use similar methods with young birds but youngsters bred in February or March are often too immature to possess the necessary sexual drive. Because of this, fanciers who want to compete at the highest level with their young birds breed them earlier to allow them further development before they are raced. Stock birds can be paired in December, with the matings timed in order to produce young birds that need to be rung by 10 January (the earliest date when the current year's rings are available). At the time of the first race these birds are about two months older than birds bred from pairings made in mid-February, and the cocks need to be separated from the young hens to prevent them from mating and producing eggs. Such early bred young cocks can be mated to older hens and the pair allowed to sit their eggs and rear youngsters. A young cock racing to eggs, or a youngster, is a formidable competitor in a race where the opposition is only motivated to fly home to its perch.

A more advanced method by which to stimulate young pigeons into better racing performances is to fool their body clocks into thinking that it is not yet time to go into a full moult. This ensures that the youngsters will be racing with a full cover of feathers whilst its competitors are suffering from the effects of a natural moult. In effect, the moult is retarded by altering the length of daylight hours that the bird experiences. Blinds are fitted to the young bird loft, and when they are closed the inside of the loft is almost completely dark. In the early part of the year, when the Spring days begin to lengthen, the blinds are closed at about 5pm and left closed until 8am, irrespective of the fact that the actual hours of daylight are much longer. This fools the pigeons into thinking that it is not yet Spring and the youngsters will go through a rapid first body moult and hold on to their wing flights until later in the season. The youngsters are kept on this system until just before the first young bird races when they are allowed natural daylight. The wing flights then begin to moult in their natural sequence, but the bird has an almost full wing for the major young bird races. There are many variations of this system and it is not advisable for the inexperienced fancier to practise it until such time as he is competent at racing birds using the natural system.

8 TRAINING AND RACING OLD BIRDS

This chapter represents the culmination of everything that has been discussed so far. The ultimate goal is to acquire a team of racing pigeons which will race successfully as they mature into older, experienced birds, and many hours of pleasure will be enjoyed by the fancier who has followed the guidelines outlined in the previous chapters. There will have been disappointments, maybe when young birds have been lost during training and racing, however the aim is success in old bird racing. Despite what is said about the pleasures of racing young birds or the excitement of timing-in a pigeon from the shorter races, these are as nothing compared to the thrill and satisfaction of timing-in a bird from a 500-mile race. Fanciers regard this type of race as the pinnacle of achievement and this is illustrated by the fact that nearly all club trophies are awarded for the longer races. Of the south road racepoints, races from the French towns of Nantes, Saintes and Pau have a mystique of their own, whilst the Scottish racepoints of Thurso, Lerwick and the Faroe Isles hold a similar fascination for fanciers flying the northern route. These races are the goals that we all aim for, and hopefully the newcomer will soon experience the great sense of satisfaction that is obtained from winning these races.

However, before such illustrious results can be achieved, the groundwork will have to be done and this chapter outlines the basic concepts which will allow the inexperienced fancier to compete with success in the old bird races. The race programme starts about the middle of April and carries on until the end of July. Racing takes place every Saturday, and there are usually about fourteen old bird races

in total followed by about eight young bird events. Often there is a gap of one or two weeks between the old and young bird races which allows the fancier to take his family on holiday or spend some time concentrating on the final stages of training the young birds.

There are also local 'open' races held before, or after, the main programme; those held previous to the main programme can be useful guides as to the readiness of the birds for the racing season proper. In theory, an open race is open to anyone, but in practice it usually means that the race is open to members of other clubs within a restricted area, such as the federation boundary. There are also numerous specialist clubs whose programmes concentrate on the longer races but the fancier needs to join a particular club before being eligible to compete. For the purpose of this book we will concentrate on the club and federation race programmes that form the backbone of pigeon racing in this country.

Preparing to Race

Before racing your old birds, your young bird team must have successfully raced the previous season, and the more confident birds who are experienced at finding their way home from distant racepoints will form the foundation of the old bird race team. In addition to these birds the loft will contain older birds that were obtained in order to breed young birds in the first year, and whilst these birds may now be flying out of the lofts they will never have received any formal training. It is possible to recruit such birds to the race team but this can only be done with limited success; the best old birds are the ones that have been raced to the loft as youngsters. There are no fixed rules in pigeon racing however, and the previous statement does not mean that all successful old birds have been raced as youngsters. This is simply a general principle, there will always be exceptions.

With limited space available, the newcomer to the sport cannot afford to house extra birds, and these non-racing birds should be kept to a minimum. In the early days of the establishment of a racing loft, the fancier should examine the results of each year's breeding, not only after the first year when the results of the young bird races are known, but each subsequent year as well, as good race birds do not always show their full potential until two or three years of age.

Many dark winter nights can be enlivened by going over breeding records and performances of offspring over several years, trying to discover that magical breeding pair which will produce winners at every mating. This careful study of breeding records will also prevent the frustration of discovering that the parents of a bird that is winning races at say, three years of age, were disposed of or lost before their full potential as breeders was recognized.

The new fancier now has a team of one-year-olds (yearlings) and these have been used to breed and rear a round of youngsters during the spring. A fancier in this situation would be foolish to treat these yearlings in the same way as the fancier with an established team of birds. In any event, yearlings need to be treated slightly differently than older birds as they are not yet fully developed and, in some respects,

Artificial eggs made from either pot or plastic.

need to be more carefully nurtured. This is so whether they are part of a balanced team of birds of different ages or a team made up solely of yearlings. Yearling pigeons can be raced with great success but they are more difficult to motivate and are often erratic in their performances. The new fancier with a team that consists only of yearlings should not attempt to win all the races in the first year, and should aim to give these birds plenty of experience in the shorter races but hold them back from the longer events. These birds are the foundation of the future racing team and if they are lost because the fancier is attempting to win longer races with yearlings, there will be no experienced birds to breed from the following year and the fancier will be back to square one.

Before the birds can be trained they need to be wing stamped and injected against paramyxovirus (see Chapter 9). The injection is a legal requirement whereas wing stamping is only required by Association rules. Both these tasks should be completed before training is started and birds should be injected against paramyxovirus more than fourteen days before the first race. The selection of birds to be raced and the completion of the entry form should be done on the night prior to basketing to allow the fancier plenty of time on Friday evening to catch and basket the birds for the race without having to rush to get to the club on time.

Training for Racing

From a pairing in mid-February, the race birds will have reared a round of young birds by the middle of March and have laid a second round of eggs by the beginning of April. Once the youngsters have been weaned the team will be ready for training for racing. It is always better, especially with yearlings, to wait until the young birds have been removed to their own compartment before training commences. It is only too easy to lose youngsters in the nest due to one of the parents spending a night out of the loft after a difficult training toss. The lone parent may not

be keen on the youngsters, or fail to keep them warm and they may die from hypothermia. A pigeon has sufficient stress when coping with the rearing of youngsters and is better left alone until this task is completed before going on to the next part of the annual programme.

Before training commences the old birds will be sitting their second round of eggs, and after ten days these eggs can be replaced with artificial ones. Pigeons raced on artificial eggs are described as being raced 'dry' and are not allowed to rear any more youngsters during that year. Sometimes, when the birds are sitting their third round of eggs, they can be motivated further by replacing one of the real eggs with an artificial substitute and allowing the other egg to hatch. Feeding one youngster does not produce such a great strain as feeding two and a yearling cock will often respond by winning races when feeding a large youngster. As the season progresses the fancier might be forced to make changes to his plans when birds are lost and new pairings have to be made to keep to the plan. The successful fancier is the one who closely studies his birds and takes advantage of every situation that arises.

For the first training toss of the season the birds should be treated in a similar manner to the young birds and taken by car for about ten miles. About fourteen days before this first toss the fancier should begin to ensure that the birds take plenty of exercise around the loft. If they are sitting or feeding youngsters they will be reluctant to exercise and it may be necessary to force them to fly. Generally, it is difficult to make hens fly when they should be sitting, and if the fancier has sufficient time he should exercise the sexes separately, hens mid-morning when the cocks have taken over the sitting duties, and cocks in the late afternoon. The birds being exercised should be locked out of the loft and, for some time, they will fly naturally, the length of the flight depending on the conditions on the day and their level of fitness. Like any athlete who has had a lay-off from training, it is necessary to build up muscle strength over a period of time rather than

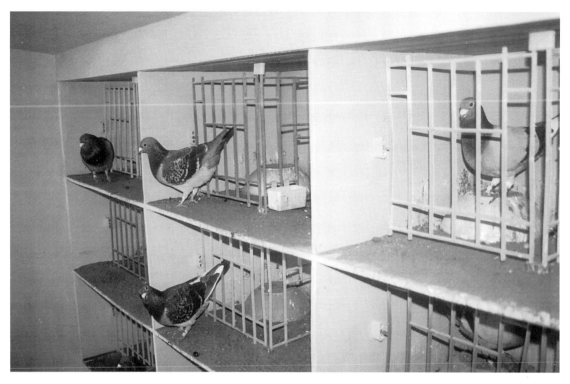

Widowhood cocks in the loft.

attempt to achieve full fitness in one training session. On the first occasion that forced flight is used the total flying time should be no more than thirty minutes. If the birds are forced to exercise when they are unfit they will only fly until they feel they have had enough and will then land on any convenient building, away from the loft – the opposite of what is required.

Forced exercise is sometimes known as 'flagging'. Fanciers often place an old piece of cloth on a pole against the loft to prevent the birds from landing. A similar 'flag' is sometimes waved about to keep the birds flying. Whatever the fancier may do, however, the birds will only fly for as long as they feel able and it is a fine art knowing just when they have had enough and when to allow them to land. Apart from fitness, weather conditions also play a part, as pigeons will fly well in clear, breezy conditions, but on murky days with little wind it is difficult to make

them fly for fifteen minutes. The general objective is to force the birds to fly for thirty minutes for several days and then gradually increase the time until they are flying well for forty-five minutes to an hour. During the racing season, even when the birds are down on eggs, it is possible to train both sexes to fly together for forty-five minutes every evening, and once they are used to this evening exercise they respond to the task with relish and will often continue with their exercise after the flag has been removed.

Pigeons which are exercising well in the manner described have little need for formal training and can be entered in the first race after only one or two training tosses by car. Exercising pigeons by 'flagging' takes up the fanciers' time but is inexpensive. As the birds get into the race programme the amount of exercise can be reduced. Once racing commences it is sufficient for them to have two weekly tosses by car providing they are exercised well every night from Monday to Thursday. If the birds are not exercising well around the loft it will be necessary to take them for plenty of tosses before the first race. Starting at about ten miles, as with the young birds, the distance should be gradually increased every day. These are experienced birds and there is no need for them to have several liberations from the same site as they are being trained solely for the purpose of getting them physically fit.

Natural Racing

As the name implies, this involves keeping the pigeons as near to nature as possible and racing them when they are either driving, sitting or rearing youngsters. As the season progresses, circumstances may occur which are out of the ordinary and the skilful fancier is the one who is aware of these and takes advantage of them. For example, a cock is missing from a race and after several days his hen leaves the nest and begins to show an interest in another cock. If her original cock returns there will be fighting between the two cocks for the hen and nestbox and eventually one of the cocks will dominate the other. It is not good practice to let them fight, although sometimes it will be impossible to stop them and pigeons rarely do serious damage to themselves when fighting. However, the original cock can be taken from the loft and placed in another compartment away from his hen and her new love. He can then be allowed to return to his hen and nestbox shortly before basketing the second cock for a race. After an initial fight the second cock is basketed but left in such a position that he can see his new hen being courted by her original cock. His jealousy spurs him to race home quickly to fight for the right to the nestbox. This is the basis of the jealousy system which is used to great effect by many fanciers.

In natural racing the birds will be particularly keen when in certain natural conditions. A cock is in his prime when sitting for about five days.

He has spent ten days driving his hen to nest and this tones up his fitness. After sitting for a few days he is at his peak and this is an ideal condition for a cock. A cock is also extra keen when he and his partner are feeding a large youngster and he is just beginning to drive his hen for their next round of eggs. Hens are always that little bit keener when sitting, and the closer the eggs are to hatching the keener the hen will be. Try putting a hand underneath a hen to check the eggs after she has been sitting for twelve days. Rather than being in fear of the fancier and getting off the nest, she will fight by striking the hand with her wing. If the eggs are beginning to chip she will be keener than ever to race home to take up her maternal duties.

Of course, if the birds are sitting artificial eggs these will never chip out, but there are tricks that can be used to fool the hen into thinking the eggs are about to hatch. Many race successes have been obtained by taking a chipping egg from another nest and placing it under the bird on artificial eggs. This can only work if the two pairs have laid at similar times as the hen will know if it is time for her eggs to hatch. A hen with eggs at the point of hatching can also be fooled by taking a newly hatched chick from another nest and placing it under the hen to be raced. As soon as the hen is basketed the chick can be returned to its own nest without any harm being done.

Although the original pairing of the natural pigeons was all done at the same time, it is better for racing if the pairs are at different stages of the nesting cycle. Generally the birds will take ten days to lay from pairing. If the first egg is laid on day ten the second will follow on day twelve. Normally the parents will not sit the first egg until the second is laid and this ensures that they both hatch on the same day. After another seventeen days from the date of the second egg (day twenty-nine) the eggs will hatch and the parent birds will begin to incubate them. If the eggs are to be replaced with artificial ones this is best done when the birds have been sitting for ten days. Obviously these eggs will not hatch, and the parents will oversit them for two or three

A widowhood cock maintaining possession of his box.

days after the time for hatching but will then give up the nest and the cock will begin to drive the hen to nest again. With natural birds it is difficult to establish exactly when the cock begins to drive, and the date on which the first egg will be laid cannot be determined accurately. If the fancier intends to enter an important race on a particular date, then it is important to be able to adjust the date of laying in order to have the hen in the best condition for the race. This is usually achieved by removing the cock, when he starts to show an interest in his hen, or by splitting the couple before the eggs have reached the date for hatching. The cock can be kept elsewhere for a few days and then re-paired to his hen in order for her to lay on the required date.

Those are a few of the examples of tricks that can be used by the natural flyer in order to increase his chances of winning races. With a long race programme the old birds may become stale through the endless routine of driving, laying and sitting, and that is the reason that many fanciers allow the pair to rear one youngster after one or two 'dry' runs. This increases the pigeons' excitement and they will regain their interest in the daily routine of the loft and bounce back into racing form. Often the cocks and hens are separated after one round of 'dry' eggs and raced for several weeks on a celibate or widowhood system, and it is this flexibility in the system that helps to keep the birds from becoming stale and leads to more successful racing performances.

Daily Planner

The following is a description of a typical week in the natural racing loft, starting on Saturday when the birds return from the race. They will be hungry but it is a mistake to allow them to feed too heavily; a seed or trapping mixture is sufficient. Such a mixture can be purchased from the corn merchant and will be specifically formulated for the purpose. It will contain numerous small seeds – red and white dari, buckwheat, sunflower, safflower, milling wheat, rape, linseed and so on, and this can be used for the bird's initial feed. The pigeons regard it as a titbit and will eat these small seeds in preference to larger grains. This mix can be given to the birds to encourage them to enter the loft or as a final 'top up' feed last thing at night. However, care should be exercised that not too much of this mixture is fed as it can lead to the birds becoming overweight. In early evening, when all the race birds are home, they should be fed lightly with a depurative mixture which is made up mainly of

barley, but also contains dari and other small seeds.

On Sunday morning the birds should be let out for exercise at their normal time but not forced to fly. Sunday is the rest day in the racing loft and the pigeons can be allowed to peck about on the lawn, build nests or chase their hens. A bath should be provided every Sunday and this should be set up outside the loft but only a few feet away. It must be emptied and cleaned out each time it is used because if the bath is left full of dirty water the birds will drink or bathe in it on other days when they should be at exercise. A strange thing about pigeons is that no matter how often the fancier provides clean drinking water for his birds they will always prefer to drink dirty water from the bath or rainwater from the house guttering. The feed on a Sunday after a race should again be a depurative mixture for both morning and evening feeds.

In the natural loft the pairs are settled in their boxes prior to laying. Note the water container is off the floor.

The pigeons should not be forced to fly during their exercise period on Monday morning and again the feed should be a depurative mixture. On Monday evening the birds should be exercised as normal and forced to fly for at least thirty minutes. The evening feed should be 50 per cent depurative with 50 per cent standard racing mixture. There are a number of formulated racing mixtures available on the market and the brand the fancier uses depends on personal preference and availability. Once a fancier has decided to use a particular racing mixture, however, it is better to stick with that mixture throughout the race season. Changes in the required diet should be brought about by adding other materials to the basic racing mixture.

On Tuesday the birds can be taken for a 20-mile training toss in the morning, which replaces their normal morning exercise. They should be fed on their return and again forced to exercise in the evening. The length of exercise time should be gradually increased during the week until the pigeons are flying for an hour each evening. A second training toss will be beneficial on either Wednesday or Thursday.

After Monday evening the feed mixture given should be the standard racing mixture. Both the amount of exercise and the length of time that the birds are kept on the depurative mixture should be varied in relation to the difficulty of the previous Saturday's race. If the birds came home at a fast speed in a tail wind they will not have used up much of their energy and should be kept on depurative until Tuesday, but if the race was hard, with a head wind, they can be put back on to the normal racing mixture on Sunday night. On Thursday the birds should be exercised as normal but should be encouraged to eat as much as possible at their evening feed. During Thursday and Friday morning a few peanuts can be fed as these are a rich source of energy and will be beneficial for the birds' performance in the Saturday race. On Friday morning the feed should be restricted and a second light meal fed at about 2pm. No other food should be given before basketing.

Widowhood Racing

Whereas the natural system of racing pigeons depends on the bird's love for its home and mate, other systems rely on the bird's sexual drive and desire to mate for motivation. Many fanciers feel that the natural system of racing pigeons is simple, whilst others consider it to be very complicated. Which system a fancier uses, or even if the fancier uses a combination of several, is a matter of personal preference, but we suggest that the newcomer to the sport should at least master the basics of the natural system before going on to something else.

In pure widowhood racing only the cocks are raced; the hens are kept in a separate loft or compartment. It is necessary to consider where the hens are to be housed during the racing season as they will need to be kept as far away from the cocks as possible. A separate loft is ideal, but this is not always possible and many fanciers make do with a compartment in the main loft. In both instances it is necessary to keep the hens out of sight of the cocks and, even better, out of hearing range. With this type of system the treatment of the hens is as important as the cocks because unless they are kept in isolation from other hens they will pair with each other and lose any sexual attraction for the cock. Some fanciers keep their widowhood hens in large aviaries and restrict their food ration to prevent them from pairing up, whilst others keep the hens in boxes specially designed for the purpose. These boxes are about twelve inches square and have a wire grille false bottom on which the bird stands. Droppings fall through the wire grille and the boxes only require cleaning once every week. Food and water are supplied by gallipots attached to the front of the box. The hens are kept in these boxes from Saturday night until the following Friday when they are put in with the cocks before they are sent to a race, although any physical contact is prevented. Widowhood hens can be let out for a fly and bath but only when their cocks are well out of the way. The principal objective of the system

Widowhood cocks at exercise.

is to prevent the cock from seeing or hearing the hen between the races.

Obviously, an essential part of this system is that the cock should have a deep affinity for his hen, and widowhood cocks are normally allowed to breed a round of youngsters in the normal manner before going on to the widowhood system. In this way a bond will have formed between the pair that will last throughout the race programme. As both cocks and hens are raced using the natural system, either one of the pair could get lost. If this happens it is then necessary to pair the remaining bird to a new partner, however this never happens with the widowhood system as only the cocks are raced.

For the fancier who is in full-time employment, widowhood can be a boon as little or no training is necessary.

Daily Planner

The following is a description of a typical week in widowhood racing, starting on Saturday afternoon when the birds return from the race. The widowhood loft will be fitted out with special widowhood nestboxes that allow the hen to be locked in one side of the box with sufficient room for the cock to stand on the outside. When the cocks are away for the race the hens will be locked in their side of the nestbox, and on the cock's return the small door in the side of the box will be opened to allow him to enter and begin to pair with his hen. The length of time that the cocks are allowed with the hens depends on the length and difficulty of the race; in short events this will only be thirty minutes whilst in longer events the cock may be left with his hen for several hours.

By nightfall on the evening following the race,

the hens will have been removed to their separate accommodation and the cocks fed with the trapping mixture and depurative mix as mentioned previously. The depurative mixture is specifically designed for widowhood racing as it will quieten the cock after the hen has been removed. Such mixtures are sometimes called 'breakdown' mixtures as they are designed to break down the protein build-up in the bird to allow him to rest and recuperate from the race. The depurative mixture is fed to the cocks for several days, and again, the number of days over which it is fed depends on the severity of the previous race. Normal feed is introduced over a couple of days and in the case of widowhood cocks this will be a specially formulated widowhood mixture which will be high in carbohydrates.

The Sunday routine is the same as for the natural pigeons except that the cocks are never forced to fly. Sunday is bath and recuperation day with the depurative mixture fed for both meals. Widowhood cocks will sulk when their hens are first taken away from them, but by Monday they will have recovered their zest and clap around the loft when they are liberated. Most of the fanciers who race widowhood cocks successfully do not train them after the first race, although they are given plenty of basket tosses beforehand. Once racing has started the cock soon learns that every time he is put into the basket he comes home to the reward of spending time with his hen.

Exercise for widowhood cocks is similar to that for natural pigeons but without the necessity of taking the pigeons by car for training tosses. Every morning the birds are let out of the loft and the doors closed and fastened to prevent the cocks from entering. The birds are locked out in this fashion for one hour, morning and night. In the early part of the week they will only fly for 15–30 minutes, but as the week moves on they will start to come into form and begin to exercise with vigour. Their manner of exercise is different from natural pigeons and they will continually land on the roof of the loft and then take off again, flying in large circles around the loft. Sometimes all the cocks will take off together and then begin to land one by one; other times they appear to want to exercise individually and will fly in their own circle round the loft. It is often the cock which flies alone when exercising that is in the best form for the forthcoming race, and it is this bird that the skilful fancier will pick as his nominated entry.

Some fanciers have developed elaborate feeding regimes for their widowhood cocks and vary the content and amount of food on various days of the week. One ounce (25g) of corn per day is often all that is allowed and this is measured out for each individual bird. Others, who are equally successful, feed the cocks in the normal type of communal feeder, but care should be taken not to overfeed. Generally, the feed intake, and in particular the intake of carbohydrates, is increased as the week progresses, with as much food as possible being crammed into the birds on the night before basketing. Of course, a pigeon will only take his fill, but pigeons that are kept hungry will gorge themselves, whereas birds that are given a full ration on a regular basis will only take what they require. Other titbits can be given to widowhood cocks and peanuts are used by many fanciers. When these are first put before the pigeons they will ignore them, but once they get a taste for them they will fight to eat as many as possible. These nuts are a good source of energy and should be used sparingly; one or two peanuts for each bird in his box after the evening feed.

The widowhood cocks should be exercised as normal from Monday morning and fastened out of the loft for one hour each morning and night. A fixed routine is important and, where possible, these exercise periods should be at the same time of day with feeding immediately afterwards. During the periods between exercise the cocks should be encouraged to rest and it will be noted that many lie down in their boxes rather than stand. The widowhood compartment should be kept in semi-darkness and the birds disturbed as little as possible. The loft should also be designed so that the birds cannot see out during the day when other pigeons flying about would disturb them.

Following the big feed on Thursday night, the cocks should only be given a light feed on Friday morning with a second light feed at about 2pm. This second feed can be supplemented with a seed or trapping mixture which will increase the bird's excitement. Shortly before basketing the hens are introduced to the cocks, but at this time the cocks are not allowed any physical contact as the hens are placed in the closed side of the nestbox with the cock on the outside. The length of time the hen should be left with the cock is a matter of debate, but it is not usually more than a few minutes. If the hens are taken by basket into the widowhood compartment and, starting at one end of the loft, placed one at a time in their boxes, by the time they have

all been boxed it will be time to start removing the first cocks and putting them into the race basket. It is most important that when the cock returns from the race his hen is in the box waiting for him, and that he is allowed access to her after he has been timed. Even the birds that are late in returning home need to receive the same treatment as, otherwise, they will lose interest and become disillusioned with the system.

Round-a-bout Racing

One of the biggest drawbacks of widowhood racing is that many good hens – potential winners – are not raced, and the fancier never knows whether a hen would have made a good

A typical race pannier designed to hold about twenty-eight race birds. Note that water troughs are available as the birds are waiting to be put on to the transporter.

racer or not. It is also necessary to keep plenty of pigeons; a team of ten cocks would require ten hens with a possible six pairs of stockbirds: thirty-two pigeons in total, housed just to race a team of ten. Using the round-a-bout system both the cocks and hens are raced and this has the advantage of increasing the number of pigeons in the race team and also testing the hens for future matings. As with widowhood, the pairs are mated before the middle of February and allowed to rear a pair of youngsters before going on to the round-a-bout system. After the youngsters have been removed and the parents are sitting their second round of eggs, the hens are again removed and placed in a separate compartment.

It is the manner in which the birds are exercised that gives the system the name 'round-a-bout', as both cocks and hens are exercised but at separate times. This system is more complicated and will certainly take up more of the fancier's time. It is essential that the loft is designed so that birds can be moved from one compartment to another without them being able to escape from the loft; a corridor at the front of the loft is the ideal solution. The hens' compartment should be as far away as possible from the cocks', and the cocks should occupy the compartment that has been used for breeding the young. The cock is treated as a widowhood cock with the exception that he is sometimes moved into the hens'

compartment whilst the hens are outside at exercise.

Firstly, the hens are exercised for one hour by shutting them out of the loft. Before they are allowed back into the loft the cocks are moved from their own section, along the corridor, to the hens' section. The traps are then opened and the hens will quickly trap and can be fed in the cocks' section. The cocks are then liberated from the hens' compartment and allowed their one hour of exercise whilst the hens are moved along the corridor to their normal section. After their exercise, the cocks are allowed back into their own section. In all other respects the pigeons are trained and fed exactly the same as widowhood cocks, but care has to be taken to prevent the hens from mating amongst themselves. This can be done by keeping their food ration to a minimum but can be counterproductive as pigeons will never be able to race if they do not receive sufficient food. Once again a balance has to be achieved and it is only by trial and error that the fancier can get this right. Other methods used to prevent hens from mating include providing only V-perches in their compartment, and having a wire grille floor. The object is to deny the hens any convenient space where they can build nests. Despite all precautions taken some hens will try to mate together and if this is observed the hens involved should be moved away and locked in individual boxes.

9 AILMENTS AND DISEASES

The most upsetting part of any livestock husbandry is coping with the variety of illnesses that might strike at any time. Experienced fanciers of many years may take these problems in their stride, but the beginner can be devastated when sickness rears its head within the flock. Treating ailments is a relatively simple matter in most cases, provided one learns to recognize and diagnose the symptoms. Before ever resorting to medical treatment one must arrive at the correct conclusion as to cause. Medical treatment can only help if the patient is rebuilt to fuller vitality and all chances of re-infection are removed – better still if the causes were avoided in the beginning. Prevention is preferable to cure but that does not mean prevention by controlled regular medical treatment, it means better awareness and attention to detail in husbandry. We do not take a painkiller because we might get a headache, we only resort to a doctor once we are sick and we certainly wouldn't dose the entire family, only the individual concerned. This should be exactly the same with livestock unless the ailment is of epidemic or threatened epidemic proportions. The following is not intended to be a treatise upon cures; that is the territory of a specialist veterinarian. It is intended as assistance towards problem recognition through elimination of possibilities, until the most probable cause and diagnosis is arrived at. The more information that the fancier can supply to the veterinarian the easier and sooner it is for him to arrive at the correct medication and cure. So many pigeon ailments have similar symptoms and yet are completely different in their nature and severity. The incorrectly prescribed antibiotic can do more long-term harm than good and overuse can exacerbate problems beyond reasonable norms.

Many common pigeon ailments are problems of equilibrium imbalance; that is to say they are stress related. Bacteria live permanently in balance within the body until something reduces the individual's vitality and the natural balance becomes upset. Constant flock treatment with antibiotics destroys this balance just as much as constant stress. They are non-selective between good and bad agents and will eventually lead to the destruction of natural balance as the recipient becomes dependent and susceptible to all manner of disease once deprived of their regular dosage. Many of the problems that arise in the novice's loft arrive through the purchase of regularly medicated stock which were dependent upon certain antibiotics at the vendor's loft but now no longer receive them. If the fancier learns to recognize the problems, many of these ailments may be prevented and in many cases they are simply cured, although in truth, the best birds in the loft never have a single day's illness in a properly run establishment.

Abdominal Trouble

See also Diarrhoea, Dropsy, Paratyphoid.

Most pigeons will display abdominal problems at some time; this does not necessarily signify disease. The most common causes of loose droppings are:

- a sudden change in air temperature from warm to cold, as pigeons fed regulated diets may use up all calorific energy to maintain body heat. This leads to mild hunger and the passing of water. The balance is soon restored with feeding

- exertion from exercise, training or racing, as once again all calorific energy has been expended, resulting in mild hunger. Again, the balance is restored with feeding
- change of feed or feeding regularity may result in the passing of wet or loose faeces until the body adjusts
- excessive use of vitamins. The metabolism will only absorb and use the minute amount required; the remainder (excess) will be expelled. Very often this expulsion is accompanied by thirst, with loose or wet faeces, and may often negate any benefit derived from vitamin addition to the diet
- toxic or deleterious substances. When the pigeon ingests anything of this nature it will immediately attempt to flush the system. Before panic measures are taken and medicine resorted to, check all possibilities and probabilities. The simple course of action that often effects a cure is to isolate the individual, and do not feed for twenty-four hours. Remove water immediately the bird has taken a drink (twice daily). On the second day, feed lightly on bulk protein and fibre (peas/beans), avoiding small grain or seeds, and remove water immediately after feeding. Gradually increase feed from the third day onwards and replace the drinker containing a proprietary enteric assisting agent, for example Entrodex. On days five, six and seven allow a course of multivitamins. Alternatively, bicarbonate of soda is an excellent calmative agent (1tbsp per 4 pints of water) during days one to three (this is also recommended for use throughout regular weekly management on one early day per week – Sunday or Monday).

The faeces from hunger/exertion/change of diet/toxins may be recognized from the following list: yellow and frothy; clear watery; water with black spaghetti-like pieces; bright green fluid; soft consistency of various colours (the colour may be dictated by diet or digestion and vary from bird to bird). Little or no odour is detectable.

Adenovirus

Now accepted as the 'young bird vomiting syndrome'. Symptoms include retention of undigested food, full crop, thirst, weight loss and foul-smelling loose faeces. It rarely affects the entire flock and the fatality rate is low; the disease may disappear almost as quickly as it arrived in individual birds or continue its infectious course through others for several days. Generally, Adenovirus is a young bird ailment and recovered birds become immune although possibly remain as carriers. It usually strikes after the first few young bird races and this suggests that the virus remains within the racing pannier after old bird racing, as it rarely attacks unflown pigeons that have reduced opportunity to come into contact with the causative virus.

Being a virus, antibiotics cannot cure it but may be used to prevent the escalation of secondary infections from stress imbalance; the most common allied secondary infections are those of a respiratory nature and E. Coli. The nursing treatment to speed recovery is as for toxin ingestion (*see* Abdominal Trouble). The period of controlled water allowance should be extended to three days, whilst feeding should remain as approximately 1oz beans/peas once per day. The antibiotic administered to best effect is Baytril. This is a Prescription Only Medicine (POM) and may only be obtained from a veterinarian upon inspection of patients. To the best of our knowledge, Baytril is not licensed for use on pigeons at this time, but a veterinarian may use this treatment at his own discretion where the patients are registered to be under his care and the fancier deemed to be trusted to follow nursing instruction implicitly.

This applies with any POM and no attempt should be made to obtain these via friends.

Further advice when using antibiotics: remove all grits and minerals; do not feed the birds any yeast-containing supplements; do not add any other additives to drinking water until the course of treatment is complete.

Anaemia

Anaemia is in the form of weakness caused by poor blood. Symptoms include pale eyes, lethargy, pallid throat and an aversion to exercise. There are several causes: non-assimilation of vitamins from natural diet; secondary reaction to many illnesses through passing of excess body fluids; old age; deficient diet; poor rearing in young birds; general debilitation from poor husbandry. The pigeons are in need of a tonic such as Cytacon B_{12}, B complex vitamins, Brewers Yeast, sulphate of iron.

Apoplexy

The symtoms of apoplexy are similar to those of paramyxovirus (PMV) – shaking, staggering, falling over, misjudging distance and collapse. It is usually only found in overheated and crowded lofts or transporters during very hot weather; overcrowding and excessive use of heating seeds or stimulants may be other causes. This is mainly a hot-weather ailment when the brain is affected by increased blood flow and rupturing of minute blood vessels causing haemorrhage. It is easily cured or rectified by increasing ventilation and darkening the loft with sun shade. Most cases demonstrate immediate recovery; the worst cases may be taken to a vet for bleeding from a wing vein. Do not attempt this yourself.

Aspergillosis

Often mistaken for canker or tuberculosis, the symptoms include a hard growth or lump in the windpipe, gasping for breath, sneezing, coughing, nasal and throat discharges, diarrhoea, swollen joints or lameness. Throat canker shows as a soft, easily removable cheesy growth; Aspergillosis is hard and embedded into tissue and cannot be removed without excessive bleeding or pain to the bird. It also attacks the liver and spleen where it may be revealed as white growths in autopsy. Infected birds are best destroyed as full recovery is unlikely.

The cause is fungus and mould spores usually floating within the immediate environment of the loft. These proliferate from damp deep litter straw or hay and lie dormant until the temperature increases. They are only one of many fungal entities lurking therein to cause a variety of illnesses. Another cause is mouldy feedstuff, such as blackened beans/peas, sour wheat/barley, powdery maize (use a magnifying glass to inspect for blue/grey mouldy powder and smell for sourness). Fumigate the loft with a mould-destroying agent, such as a Greenhouse smoke bomb (remove all birds), and sterilize all drinkers, grit boxes, corn bins and so on.

Valuable stock may be treated although this is very time consuming: paint a solution of aqueous iodine, glycerine and honey on to the affected throat area with an artist's brush. This solution must also be added to the drinking water for patient and uninfected birds alike. There is no guaranteed cure and vital organ damage will remain permanently.

Ataxia

This is a lack of co-ordinated movement due to a fault in the nervous system. Ataxia is hereditary and could be mistaken for Paramyxovirus (PMV), although no other symptoms are shown. It is undesirable in racing pigeons although it is demonstrated in some fancy show breeds, for example Broad Tailed Shakers, Show Fantails and Tipplers. It is rare in racing pigeon families and best if eliminated.

Bone Troubles

For example: Bent Keel, Rickets, 'Off Legs Syndrome'.

Bent Keels in squeakers are usually caused by pressure upon the soft cartilaginous-type bone before hardening and not always through lack of calcium as is sometimes thought. This can be avoided by checking nesting materials for depth and comfort as the full weight of the squab is borne upon its keel. Always wean the birds into deep dry straw for the first few days and avoid perching opportunities on hard edges.

Rickets are caused by lack of sufficient calcium and trace elements. Any loft that ensures an adequate supply of fresh grits and minerals daily should not have any cases of rickets. Some birds are unable to assimilate these into the metabolism from feed or supple-ments however, and draw their requirement from their own bones. If bone weakness persists after supplementation then it must be deemed to be an undesirable fault.

'Off Legs Syndrome' is caused by a variety of things:

*   insufficient calcium and trace elements in the diet. Laying hens draw these from their bones to provide shell to eggs, so ensure adequate feed content
*   excess weight causing pressure to nerve endings. Reduce feed slightly but maintain quality
*   lack of iron, causing anaemia. Give the birds Cytacon B_{12}, or B complex (no more than twice weekly). Do not give Brewers Yeast to parents rearing young due to possible yeast/fungus problems and ignore

The result of an attack by depluming mites is a condition known as 'feather rot' which can also be caused by a fungal infection at the base of the feather.

any recommendation to do so! Although Brewers Yeast is an excellent weapon in the pigeon fancier's armoury for supplying B Complex vitamins, there are times when it must not be used, for example during rearing whilst administering antibiotic treatments, or when nursing pigeons with fungal afflictions.

Canker (Trichomoniasis)

Pigeons have this permanently and will maintain equilibrium until severely stressed. There are two main forms and over forty strains of common infectious protozoa.

With throat canker a soft cheesy growth forms and may be easily removed with a cotton bud dipped in aqueous iodine and glycerine, then treated with a standard veterinary cure. Internal cankers affecting various organs and mucosa are treated immediately with veterinary products. All infected birds should be isolated as it is readily spread to any bird in low condition via the feed or drinkers. Canker does not require routine treatment but may be monitored by regular clinical inspection of faeces and treated only as required. Canker equilibrium imbalance is often a secondary infection to more serious disease and an ideal monitor of general health. Therefore it does not make sense to attempt to completely eradicate this protozoan with routine flock treatment, but only to maintain a natural equilibrium within the immune system. Only treat badly infected (imbalanced) birds; they can be cured within three to five days plus three to five days convalescence.

Catarrh (Coryza-Mycoplasmosis)

See also Ornithosis and Psittacosis.

Symptoms include clear watery discharge from eyes, nostrils and throat and wheezing or rattling sounds when breathing. This is yet another equilibrium disorder; pigeons live permanently with the causative agent and there will never be a total cure. However, it may be treated with antibiotics when taking a severe form. There is absolutely no need to treat as routine; we do not treat ourselves as routine for the common cold and that is exactly what this is! However, an athlete may take an expectorant (mainly garlic based) and there are products of this nature available for pigeons.

The most common afflictions to cause problems are as follows.

One-Eyed Cold

This takes several forms, some innocuous and some pernicious (the symptom of more serious disease). One-Eyed Cold in young birds often ties in with peak moulting time, coinciding with a wide variation in atmospheric temperature (hot days and cold nights). Generally speaking, this is easily rectified by greater ventilation or isolation to an aviary and increasing Vitamin C supplement. Left to take its course the patient recovers in four to seven days and gentle swabbing of the eye to remove dried particles certainly helps. In the old days fanciers would spit in the bird's eye as saliva contains a natural antiseptic as the body's primary defence against infection. This is not to be recommended if one smokes or carries an infectious disease, but is not as ludicrous as it sounds (notice how quickly a wound heals when licked?).

One-Eyed Cold is identified by clear water and air bubbles in one eye only, accompanied by slight swelling and reddening of eyelid and cere. Should these symptoms develop to dark reddening and hard mucous deposits plus nasal discharge and severe breathing problems, then the bird has a more serious disease.

Protein Poisoning

Never covered by veterinarians, this may often be a problem and young birds definitely benefit from a lighter diet during the warmer months.

Allergy

In some cases pigeons are allergic to the loft environment or other inmates. Once isolated to a solitary cell, cure is effected almost immediately.

Vitamin Deficiency

Stress from moulting, training and racing makes great demands on the bird and insufficient vitamins may be assimilated into the body from feed to maintain balance.

Catarrh

A rattling and heavy wheezing in an otherwise healthy bird may be cured by POM injectable Oxytetracycline, into the subcutaneous tissue of the neck (by fancier) or into breast muscle (by veterinarian). One shot only is required to effect cure, coupled with aviary convalescence. Convalescent birds should receive honey and garlic plus additional vitamin C in drinking water and probiotic to speed recovery. That is the way to use antibiotics: an individual dose for an individual patient, without flock-treating healthy birds.

Dry Cold

Very often, when fanciers suspect respiratory problems they immediately reach for antibiotics and are baffled when no cure is forthcoming. Little wonder, because very few of them actually know anything about this problem. Dry cold is rather like hay-fever in humans – sneezing, breathing difficulties, and yet perfectly healthy in all other respects. The cause is most probably lack of humidity and air circulation during dry spells, or lack of air circulation within an excessively closed loft environment coupled with overcrowding. All lofts should have at least two cubic metres (70cu ft) of moving air space per bird.

To detect a dry cold, first gently press upon each side of the wattles with finger and thumb; the bird will sneeze. Inspect under the wattle and one will observe a blunt needle-like appendage. This is the incumbent valve and serves a function similar to hair in the human nostril, preventing dust and so on from entering and blocking the airway. In the unaffected bird this should appear slightly moist (not wet) and clear, being a healthy pink.

The affected bird will react differently; when applying slight pressure to the wattles, instead of sneezing, the pigeon will awkwardly open its beak and attempt to shake its head. The incumbent valve will appear dry and powdery with slight deposits of dust and mucus. The pigeon will only breath through its beak and any attempt to close the slight gap will meet with resistance. The inside of the wattle must be gently cleaned with a slightly moistened feather taking care to remove any deposits. Remove all dust from the loft and increase humidity (put in an extra drinker). There are expectorant-type products on the pigeon market for keeping the birds airways clear. Most importantly, do not overcrowd and reduce the dust as much as possible. This is the most common respiratory problem and antibiotics are not required nor will they cure.

Chlamidospore

See also Aspergillosis, Psittacosis, Ornithosis, Thrush (Candida Albicans).

These are airborne fungus spores, asexually produced from a portion of the cell and able to survive in unfavourable conditions when the fungus itself may be killed. Usually found in conjunction with Mycoplasmas, E. Coli, Pneumonococcus, and so on. Chlamidias are treated as a virus, but in some cases may be cured with antibiotics where a virus cannot. In layman's terms they are midway between virus and bacteria.

Cuts

Wash cuts clean with a mild antiseptic and dress with Acriflavin or paint with Lugols Iodine. If there is damage to eye ceres, wash with clean water only (boiled and cooled) and leave to dry, do not use any antiseptic that might cause irritation or eye damage.

Diarrhoea

This is a symptom rather than a disease and may indicate disease of an enteric nature. It may be caused by a number of factors:

- arsenic, copper, lead poisoning from pesticides, for example
- a change of diet or an impoverished diet
- hunger
- stress from exertion (from training/racing)
- reaction to medication or additives
- excess vitamins
- medical activities to galvanized drinking vessel causing chemical reaction
- drinking water from garlic (never leave to stand in a galvanized container, use fresh crushed cloves each time)
- algae build-up in hosepipes used for filling drinkers and so on
- a sudden drop in air temperature.

If the faeces is devoid of odour it is only a metabolic imbalance – provide more fibre/protein in the diet, and bicarbonate of soda in water or use Entrodex and electrolytes for rehydration. Should the faeces be foul-smelling, unusually coloured or blood-spattered, use the check list in this chapter to assess other disease probabilities. The pigeon will always try to physic itself by flushing out its system; in some respects this is good, but the danger lies in cross-infection of other loft inmates when normally harmless bacteria can flare into problematic increased activity. Always isolate suspected sick birds immediately to prevent further spread – better safe than sorry!

Dropsy

This is usually a problem with older hen pigeons, which will demonstrate a swollen abdomen filled with watery tissue. The bird gasps for breath with constant panting and signs of exhaustion. There are several causes – obesity at laying; lack of exercise; overbreeding; weak heart; worms (severe); coccidiosis; digestive problems; injury and internal tumour. Birds rarely recover and may be barren. Cock birds will never attain full vigour and will usually be infertile.

Egg Bound

This is more common than dropsy and can affect hen pigeons of all ages: the pigeon is unable to pass the egg due to obesity or reduced condition. In some cases the egg is being miscarried or aborted whilst at the soft shell stage. This happens when the female has started into egg production but contact with a mate has ceased (male or female), and they have neglected to consume sufficient food or grit. For want of a better analogy, the hen is heartbroken! In both cases the egg will require surgical removal or nursing assistance, taking care not to break a shelled egg internally. This may be done by using your vaccination syringe (without needle) to insert warm olive oil (at body temperature) into the vent and leaving nature to take its course after applying very gentle massage. With the soft variety, do not apply massage. The process may need to be repeated two to three times.

Most hens recover from the experience, although in many cases they do become reluctant layers and in some cases it may signify the onset of infertility or barrenness. Should there also be tumours present, benign or malignant, then no amount of care will restore the pigeon to perfection.

Enteritis

See also Ornithosis, Psittacosis, Canker, Paratyphoid (Salmonellosis).

Inflammation of the mucous membrane of the intestine, the symptoms being watery droppings, weakness or listlessness, poor appetite and excessive thirst, and possibly blood specks in faeces. It may be caused by bad digestion, severe worm infection or rodent contamination of feed, and lead to liver damage and problems in other vital organs, depending on the causative organism. Simple cases may be nursed and convalesced in a similar manner to diarrhoea, whilst severe cases require veterinary consultation.

Epilepsy

Sporadic convulsions without the appearance of ill health. This is genetic and mainly found in fancy breeds. It is undesirable in racing pigeons as there is no cure.

Feather Rot

There are two causes of feather rot: fungus and a feather-boring mite. Both cases thrive in damp, for example residual damp from faeces on perches/nests/floor corners. It is usually found to affect birds of the coarse-webbed feather-type. The fungus, microbe or mite lives within the soft pulp of the feather shaft, gradually breaking it to stubble until bald patches appear. Affected pigeons may be bathed in camphor water, or alternatively use a proprietary specific to feather rot. Pigeons will moult clean, but the problem may reoccur at the next humid season.

In earlier times, fanciers applied crushed mothballs and soap to the infected area or painted it with paraffin oil. The modern veterinary treatment is injectable using Ivomec, which also acts as a complete de-louser and wormer. This injection must be done under veterinary instruction only. Ivomec has proved safe for pigeons and has also shown a capability

A bad infection of canker or trichomoniasis in the throat of a young bird. Although the condition can be treated, this bird was unable to feed and had to be suppressed.

to improve feather quality at subsequent moulting. There are other products available, however these are not licensed for use on pigeons and are therefore not recommended.

Fungus

See also Aspergillosis, Chlamidospore, Feather Rot, Thrush (Candida Albicans).

Fungal disorders in pigeons are not always readily recognized until their manifestation into more serious illnesses. These take numerous forms and reduce resistance to secondary infections. Fungal disorders attack the respiratory system, nervous system, reproductive organs and air sacs, reducing performance and yet the bird often displays apparent health. The causes are outlined under the various disease headings but a couple of extra causes are outlined below.

Aflatoxin Poisoning

Aflatoxin is produced by a mould (*Aspergillus flavus*) which may develop in any badly harvested or stored grain or vegetable matter (straw, hay, and so on). The mould thrives upon changeable humidity when the grain (or growing plant) is exposed to warmth after damp conditions.

Unfortunately, Aflatoxin develops unseen within the centre of the grain; outwardly the feedstuff has the appearance of being sound. Seasonal weather, incorrect storage plus several other factors may promote the fungal growth, one of which could be condensation within the silo or the corn bin. Aflatoxin poisoning can result in brain, lung, heart, liver, spleen and kidney damage, and at its least, severe loss of condition, at its worst sudden death.

Aspergillus attacks birds more easily than humans, although research into pigeons and poultry is ongoing. One of the main causes is mouldy maize or peanuts which are two main components of the pigeon diet. Maize should be scrutinized regularly and peanuts purchased as fit for human consumption; they should be purchased and fed in small amounts due to their fickle storability.

Another cause of fungal disorder may lie within loft management, for example damp hay or straw – not necessarily damp within the fancier's loft but dampened and dried before purchase. A further cause comes via the addition of Brewers Yeast to feed whilst treating with antibiotics (the fancier is adding a mould to a mould and in many cases negating the medical treatment). Fortunately most mild fungal disorders can be controlled by the addition of Lugols aqueous iodine to the water and this may also have a tonic effect when not abused (1tsp per gallon). More serious problems require veterinary identification and treatment. Sometimes the symptoms of fungal problems may be mistaken for those of PMV.

Gapes

Not as common today as in years gone by, mainly due to the fact that people no longer keep pigeons and poultry together, as well as better kept surrounding loft areas. The symptoms of Gapes are: gasping for breath, head shaking and coughing without any sign of apparent illness. This is caused by the Gape worm (*Syngamus trachaelis*) which develops inside another host, for example an earthworm, maggot or snail, that thrives around soiled ground near poultry, ducks and geese. Once ingested, the parasitic worm feeds in the lung on blood for ten days, then makes its way after rapid growth to the windpipe. The adult male attaches itself to the female forming a letter 'Y', causing the bird to gasp or 'gape' when it is eventually coughed up on to the ground or into water. Mainly a farmyard or smallholding pest; don't keep your bantams, Muscovy ducks, and so on in close proximity to pigeons!

Going-Light

Once again, this is a symptom rather than an illness and may be related to a number of causes. The bird suffers rapid weight loss, listlessness and emaciation. Possibly caused by coccidiosis, ornithosis, psittacosis, fungal related disorder, canker etc. In this instance, consult a vet.

There is a second form of going-light which is more common than supposed. This is when an apparently healthy bird with a full body handles extremely light (not fit and corky), seems to lack vitality, will not fly and when made to do so appears to be 'all in'. Often these birds will rarely leave the loft floor or struggle to reach their perch, and seem lifeless in the hand. This could be due to having been entered into a race whilst not fully fit and that race proving to be extremely hard. The bird could be suffering from overexertion, with all will and physical power destroyed, and the bird may never recover its former character. Another cause could be competing immediately after medication or whilst fighting some unnoticed ailment. Whatever the cause, for the sake of the pigeon, do not race it again and monitor all offspring for signs of vigour loss!

Indigestion

The pigeon may fail to digest its full feed overnight, possibly as a result of:

- gorging after hunger
- the grain being kiln dried and too hard to soak and digest
- too much barley
- irregular feeding
- overfeeding directly after competition or difficult race
- lack of grit in gizzard.

The bird should be allowed to convalesce, with food provided sparingly then gradually building-up in quantity. Replenish fresh clean grits and minerals, and include bicarbonate of soda in the drinker. If the ailment persists, consult a vet as one other possibility may be that the pigeon has a hernia of the gizzard for which there is no cure.

Lameness

This could result from an injury, Staphylococcus Arthritis, Aspergillosis, Tuberculosis or Salmonella Typhymurium. Consult a vet if the bird is not obviously injured. If the lameness is a result of disease, a penicillin injection may be required.

Liver Problems

Symptoms include consistent yellow fluid droppings, lassitude and thirst. This may be attributed to genetic fault; overuse of vitamins A and D; lack of sunshine; damp; lack of exercise; long periods of imprisonment; damage from previous disease; excessive use of stimulants or incorrect use of antibiotics (overdose). Allow the bird plenty of sunshine and exercise, and cut down any excess use of cod liver oil or multi-vitamins.

Megrins

Symptoms are similar to those of PMV, Paratyphoid, Salmonellosis, Ataxia and some fungal disorders – staggering; loss of coordination; dizziness; nervousness; neck torsion; and crashing into walls. The cause is unidentified; it is possibly due to cross infection from wild birds, contaminated feed or it may be hereditary. There is no known cure.

Newcastle Disease

This is the poultry equivalent of Paramyxovirus. Although not entirely identical, both are caused by identified virus PMV1. Newcastle Disease sufferers do not recover fully and remain as carriers. All stock must be destroyed and burned. It is highly contagious and may be carried place to place by contacts. It is not infectious for humans but may be carried on clothing, and so on. Insufficient is known about the disease in relation to pigeons but, due to its relationship with PMV, it is treated similarly.

Ornithosis

See also Pneumonia.

Caused by the bacteria *Microbacterium multiforme* and found in pigeons and other domestic or wild birds and animals. General symptoms are as described for Catarrh. Further symptoms include matting of the eyes; constant nasal discharge; hunched up appearance; raised feathers on rump; damp matted patches upon wing butts (from eye-wiping or scratching); constant sneezing.

It is highly contagious, and similar to Psittacosis but more common and less harmful to man. Veterinary diagnosis is required to differentiate it from Psittacosis and treatment is not recommended. Damage to all vital organs, possible blindness or impaired vision and weakness may remain following the disease. Cured birds never make satisfactory racers or breeders and may remain as carriers.

It is extremely difficult to eradicate and may recur. Try to avoid this by destroying and burning all infected birds, completely isolating all others into fresh air aviary quarantine, and disinfecting the loft and all utensils; blow torch and disinfect the loft again and limewash it. It is essentially a filth disease; the most likely cause is cross infection from wild birds.

Paramyxovirus

Caused by a strain of PMV1, of which there are many strains and various degrees of virulence. Symptoms are many and varied and may appear together or alone. They include watery faeces; slimy green and brown faeces; nervousness; lack of co-ordination; falling backwards; misjudging distance; fear of sudden noise; reaction to bright light; neck torsion; complete twisting movement of neck; and inability to pick up grain

immediately. There is no cure but recovery occurs after nursing and convalescence for 10–14 weeks. The mortality rate is dependent upon the viral strain contracted; some strains may kill within days, but this is extremely rare. Most strains result in recovery and future immunity for the individual, although some may demonstrate continued nervousness for up to two years. Parental immunity cannot be transferred to young so natural immunity is impossible. Some immune individuals may become susceptible once again after several years of non-contact; the immune system rejects unused or unrequired defences periodically, whilst updating its armoury.

The disease has an incubation period of 8–12 weeks after which the symptoms begin to appear. During this period the pigeons are infectious to others. The symptoms are actually the onset of recovery which takes another 8–14 weeks, plus further convalescence before the bird may be raced with confidence. Immunity is passed from immune parent to nestlings, however this immunity only lasts for three weeks and youngsters should be vaccinated at 21–28 days old. Prevention is via vaccination for both young and old but fourteen days must be allowed for the vaccination to become effective; immunity is not immediate and also builds and wanes over a period of ten months' full effectiveness (not twelve months as many imagine).

Not all pigeons contract Paramyxovirus; some are resistant, possibly due to having contracted a mild but unnoticed strain at some previous time. However, this is not an argument for non-vaccination. Experience of this disease is extremely distressing and annual preventative vaccination of all owned pigeons is to be desired, and is a legal requirement in all EU countries. The disease may be spread as airborne, fancier-borne or contact-borne, so aviary prisoner stock are not exempt from risk. Vaccination is ineffective against the disease once the pigeon is in the stages of incubation of the virus. Recovered birds do not remain as carriers of the present pigeon-related strain of

PMV, however viruses do mutate so all information available may be subject to revision in future.

Paratyphoid (Salmonellosis)

Squeakers may suddenly lose weight at 4–6 weeks and display staring eyes; twisting necks; loss of balance; gasping; difficulty in eating or digesting; mainly water-filled crop; unwillingness to fly up to perches. Old birds demonstrate dropped wing; wing swelling; lameness; swollen foot (usually left foot). Hens become barren, and their eggs fail to hatch. Infected pigeons may show any or all of the symptoms; carriers rarely show any symptoms at all. The complexity of correct diagnosis makes this the fanciers' most common but often wrongly diagnosed illness. The many and varied symptoms cause confusion for treatment, but are actually good signs for diagnosis when several birds appear to be ailing in different ways. The greatest problem is in identifying the carrier which may appear fully fit.

The main causes are rodent-contaminated feed, and cross infection from wild birds or contact with a carrier from elsewhere. Fanciers often confuse this disease with PMV due to the similarity of symptoms, hence the fanciers who claim their pigeons contacted PMV after vaccination. Treated under veterinary supervision cure is possible, however some birds may remain as future carriers so the problem may continue until all carriers are lost or destroyed.

Pigeon Pox

First noticed in pigeons during the late 1800s/early 1900s, and originating in southeast Asia and spreading through Europe via importation of various bird species. All birds carry the pathogen/pox virus. Symptoms are scabby lesions upon exposed skin areas such as

the legs, ceres, or the mucous membrane of the beak. The pathogen is carried on the dust of dried faeces, nasal discharge, ticks, mites, flies and contacts, generally entering the host body via cuts or abrasions and incubating for 2–3 weeks before manifesting as lesions or scabs. Infected birds may be infectious to others throughout the cycle which invariably runs a 6–8-week course.

Recovered pigeons are later immune for life and do not remain as carriers, however it is usual for other secondary infections to be present at the time and these may require treatment to speed the birds' recovery. From a fancier's point of view the disease is a nuisance to be avoided during the racing season, and this may be achieved via vaccination and non-contact for three weeks with pigeons from other lofts. Unfortunately vaccinated birds do not have lifetime immunity and must have repeat treatment.

Pneumonia

A secondary infection usually accompanying Ornithosis, Psittacosis or Cold. It is caused or spread via dust-infected dried droppings (faeces), contact, feed trays or drinkers. There are two types of pneumonia: Virus and Pneumonacoccus. There is no cure, and it is best to cull at the first sign; fanciers who do so seldom have future problems. Pigeons that easily succumb to secondary infections usually die before veterinary diagnosis or treatment is possible, as these secondary infections may include several simultaneously.

Prolapse

A displaced oviduct or rectum protruding from the vent after egg-laying, after which the pigeon's future as either a racer or breeder is doubtful. Usually caused by obesity, over-breeding or old age. The protruding organ may be gently replaced with gentle coercion but is liable to infection if not immediately noticed.

Psittacosis (parrot fever)

A viral disease similar to Paratyphoid, usually affecting young birds. Symptoms include pasty and sticky mucus in throat lining and mouth; diarrhoea; green and white faeces (smelly); soiled, matted vent; swollen abdomen; vomiting; poor appetite; listlessness; panting; rump may be seen to constantly rise and fall; dull, partially closed eyes; sneezing. Weaned birds tend to stay upon the loft floor, and look a pitiful sight. The birds usually die in the nest, and death is fairly rapid to older, infected birds. Caused by virus passed via sneezing, faeces, food contamination, and so on.

The incubation period is 2–10 days, and onset is very sudden with a high fatality rate. It is usually accompanied by various secondary infections, such as Canker, Pneumonia, Peritonitis (liver and kidney infection), Enteritis, Roup; pus forming in air sacs and lungs; damage to heart, liver, kidneys and spleen. Birds that contract a mild form survive to become carriers. Destroy and burn all infected stock and disinfect all loft fixtures and fittings. Survivors with immunity can be distinguished by a blood test taken from a wing vein by the veterinarian. Those not showing immunity from previous infection may be vaccinated by the vet.

Psittacosis is essentially a filth disease caused by damp and wet droppings. If you smell ammonia or foul odour and house flies are in abundance, then suspect the onset of disease. Pigeons will very often eat maggots that may be contaminated.

Renal Disease

A disease of the kidney and intestine, mainly affecting old prisoner stock. It is rare in a racing loft, although possibly a cause of sudden death.

Kidney stones or kidney failure may be found in an autopsy.

Respiratory Disease

See also Cold, Roup.

This comes in a variety of forms: bacterial, fungal, toxin ingestion and viral. More severe cases usually occur as a secondary infection. All pigeons carry the pathogen for colds and under normal circumstances are resistant. Viral forms are controlled but not cured by antibiotics; the drug is only effective against bacterial secondary infections. These are administered as assisting agents to the immune system and not against the virus itself over which they have no effect. Identify the disease before administering antibiotics. Many respiratory disorders may be cured (a misnomer), relieved (more accurate description) and health improved by fresh air, isolation and better loft hygiene.

Rickets

See also Bone Troubles.

Caused by lack of calcium, damp conditions, inattentive parents or an impoverished diet, and followed by arthritis or rheumatic condition with permanent weakening of muscular efficiency. It is best to cull affected squabs. Separate the parents and rebuild a vigorous condition in each before remating for breeding purposes.

Roup

A highly contagious form of avian diptheria. Symptoms include cold; running nostril; mucous; inflamed eyes; catarrh; dry cheesy matter in throat and nostrils; sometimes pox-like lesions; bluey-grey membrane in throat and on tongue; and grey-coloured wattles. Consult a vet and treat as a respiratory infection. Isolate patients, increase ventilation, fumigate the loft and convalesce all birds in an open air environment as much as possible. Mainly caused by overcrowding and bad ventilation or cross infection from wild birds.

Scaly Leg (Mange)

Caused by the mite *Sarcoptens gallinae mutans*. Wash legs in paraffin and paint with iodine and vaseline.

Thrush

A fungal disorder (*Candida albicans*) normally in equilibrium but increased by stress. Causes include mouldy feed, and spores from droppings or litter. It may attack the throat, respiratory tracts, reproductive organs and vent, and is more common in nestlings. Symptoms include grey-coated throat; blue-coated tongue (do not confuse with blue-tipped tongue which is inherited pigmentation not a disease symptom); rattling and general debilitation or poor growth. Old pigeons show lack of vigour, reluctance to mate or rear young, may refuse to feed infected young, and change nest location where possible. The cure for old pigeons is to swab the throat with a mixture of aqueous iodine, glycerine and honey. Use water purifier in drinkers, blow torch dry any damp nesting areas and disinfect. Check all feed for sourness. There is no worthwhile cure for nestlings. The worst case scenario is that Thrush can escalate via secondary complications into Aspergillosis or Psittacosis. Identify immediately and effect prompt action. It is not serious if caught immediately.

Trichomoniasis

See Canker.

Vertigo

Old name for Paramyxovirus.

Worms

Treat as required with proprietary recognized wormer. There are many types, so have faecal tests on suspicion of infestation. It may be treated routinely pre-season, and garlic is a useful preventative agent.

We hope this list of ailments will prove useful to novices and experienced fanciers alike. These are the main problems within the pigeon loft, and no matter how good the general management, some will eventually be encountered. Diseases such as E. Coli and Rotavirus may be present at the same time and are generally treated as part of disease medication en bloc. Treatment with antibiotics must be under veterinary supervision only and not on the recommendation of friends; because of the variety of strains of any singular infection, the preventative and curative treatment may vary from loft to loft, area to area. The name of an antibiotic is the copyright licence of the pharmaceutical company; a different name does not necessarily mean a different drug and therefore both could prove to be unsuccessful. Different drugs work upon different bugs so it is imperative that the correct drug for the prevailing strain of bug be used, and only an up-to-date veterinarian will know the best option.

In modern pigeon racing it is becoming universally accepted practice for fanciers to have swab (blood of faeces (droppings)) tests performed by veterinary laboratories. This is a good practice and relatively cost effective, however on occasions fanciers are mystified by some of the professional jargon and are completely in the dark should no curative advice be supplied along with diagnosis. This is frustrating, but many of the findings are part and parcel of a particular debilitating illness and treatment is afforded by a broad spectrum of medicines for these secondary infections at the same time.

It must also be borne in mind that any treatment via medication introduces a further stress of its own. This stress is caused by interference with the normally natural balance of good–bad agents within the immune system. Broad spectrum medicines are non-selective and will on occasion be a non-requisite part of treatment, where the veterinarian might consider the situation best left to run its course of natural healing. Some diseases are better if not totally eradicated because they act as monitors for the general overall condition of individuals and the flock. Amongst these are Coccidiosis and Trichomoniasis (Canker), along with some fungal disorders that are naturally present.

GLOSSARY

'Bastard' Wing Consists of one main feather overlaid by one or two smaller feathers to give it rigidity. When in danger of stalling, the pigeon spreads this, allowing the airflow to be restored.

'Bobwires' A system of wires placed at the entrance to the loft that will only open inwards.

Breed The racing pigeon is a breed of pigeon. Different types within the breed are referred to as strains.

Cere The area around the eye that is devoid of feathers. The texture and size varies considerably with the age of the bird, its sex and strain.

Circle Describes the flight of the pigeon when it leaves the loft.

Clocked When the thimble containing the race rubber is put into the clock and the clock lever is depressed.

Convoy A number of birds from different organizations being transported to the race-point.

Convoyer The licensed official who is in charge of the convoy and responsible for safe liberation.

Cote As in 'dovecote'. The structure in which pigeons are housed. *See also* kit or loft.

Covers The small feathers that cover the flesh and lower parts of the flights.

Crooked Keel A condition where the breast-bone or 'keel' develops a twist instead of being straight. It can be caused by bad diet or unsuitable bedding.

Crop 'Milk' A protein and fat mix produced by parents for feeding their young.

'Dead in Shell' The condition where a youngster dies at the point of breaking out from the shell.

Deep Litter A deep covering of the loft floor with material such as straw or wood shavings.

Drag The pull of the majority of racing birds in one direction, to the detriment of lofts situated in another direction.

Driving The beginning of the mating ritual when the cock lowers his tail and sweeps the floor as he pursues the hen.

Dropboard A level board fixed to the ouside of the loft on which the pigeon can land. *See also* landing board.

Egg Tooth Situated on top of the beak of the embryo, it is used to rip the egg shell membrane so that the youngster can break out.

Flagging A method of forcing exercise by waving a pole with a piece of cloth attached.

Flights The main feathers of the wing and tail.

Flyaway The loss of a group of youngsters, en masse, when they roam too far away from the loft and become lost.

Fret Mark A fault in the feather caused by stress or a sudden lack of food supply when the feather was being grown.

Handling The correct way to hold a pigeon, combined with a series of movements to enable the fancier to assess the bird's condition using the sense of touch.

Hopper   A communal feeder.

Kit   The structure in which pigeons are housed. *See also* cote or loft.

Landing Board   A level board fixed to the outside of the loft on which the pigeon can land. *See also* dropboard.

Latebred   A young bird bred late in the year and too young to participate in the young bird races.

Lib-Line   The telephone information service supplied by *British Homing World* to give liberation news.

Line of Flight   The anticipated line of flight from the liberation site to the home loft.

Loft   The structure in which pigeons are housed. *See also* cote or kit.

'Night Out'   An expression used to describe the situation where a pigeon fails to reach its home loft on the day of liberation.

Pan-tiles   Domestic roofing tiles used to cover a pigeon loft roof, which also allow a flow of air between the tiles.

Pooling   The gambling system used in pigeon racing.

Primaries   The large main wing feathers, ten in total.

Ringer   The instrument used to expand the race rubber, allowing it to be placed on the bird's leg.

Rubber   A rubber race ring.

Sealing Pliers   An instrument used to close the numbered seal on to the string securing the clock or race pannier.

Secondaries   The smaller main wing feathers, ten in total.

Sputnik   A specially designed trap to enable the pigeon to enter the loft directly.

Squeaker   A young pigeon in the weeks before it can fly, so named due to the noise it makes.

Strains   Different types of pigeon within the breed known as racing pigeons.

Strike   The action of activating all clocks simultaneously against the master timer.

Sweeps   Short-distance racing popular at the beginning of the twentieth century.

Thimble   The receptacle into which the race rubber is inserted before it can be put into the clock.

Tic bean   A small, round bean grown widely in Europe as food for cattle or sheep, but also ideal food for pigeons.

Toss   The action of liberating birds for a training flight.

Wattle   The white, crusty growth above the beak. The size and structure varies widely between strains.

INDEX